New Studies for Women
on Living in the Spirit

Betty Jane Grams
WOMEN OF GRACE

C0-AYG-262

Radiant BOOKS
Gospel Publishing House/Springfield, Mo 65802

02-0751

WOMEN OF GRACE

Library of Congress Catalog Card Number 77-93409
ISBN 0-88243-751-8
Printed in the United States of America
3rd Printing 1980

A leader's guide for individual or group study with this book is available from the Gospel Publishing House (order number 32-0226).

Contents

Foreword

A Book Especially for Women

"Our women are reading all kinds of books; studying all kinds of different studies. When are we going to prepare something for our own women?" This question from a friend rang a bell in my heart. It echoed similar questions we had heard following the women's leadership retreats in Chile and Argentina.

This book was born of a felt need. The seeds were planted as we visited some 200 pastors' homes during each furlough. Mothers and wives would talk to me. Young people opened their hearts to me. I heard the queries. I saw the need in the homes for learning to *live* what we believe; to translate the concepts of God's Word into our daily living and bear fruit. I saw the need to actually be like Christ in our daily life.

True, we worship in Pentecostal churches, churches of the Holy Spirit. Gifts of the Spirit are manifested in our services. This is our distinctive testimony, the riches of our inheritance, a Spirit-filled life.

We feel there are important guidelines that can draw women into a Spirit-anointed life and a ministry. We see and exercise the gifts of tongues and interpretation, as well as the gift of prophecy, corroborating the preaching of the Word. We need to consider the fruit of the Spirit, which should begin to grow in our lives the moment we accept Christ into our hearts.

We are made new creatures in Christ Jesus. The old life, old thoughts, old desires, and old ways of reacting have passed away; we live and act in a new way. We walk in the Spirit and are gently led by Him.

Many years ago I heard my old German father-in-law speak about a neighbor who liked to testify a lot at church. Unimpressed, he said, "You vil notice dat his vife and children do look at the floor."

At home in front of her husband and children, a woman is transparent. Too many young people have said to me, "If only my mother would have lived at home what she testified at church and at the WM meetings . . . ." We must be willing to grow and change as the Spirit leads so we can show our children what Christ is like.

It is significant that the Holy Spirit is guiding us in our first women's Bible study book to study who we *are,* rather than what we can *do.* We will focus on what kind of persons we are intrinsically, rather than on what our ministry will be. The Holy Spirit wants to help us have fruit that grows. This calls for constant development of Christlikeness in our lives. Then we will truly be women of grace, attracting others to the Lord.

As the fruit of the Spirit develops within us, we can share that fruit with our families, neighbors, church, and world.

Let me relate to you some women's testimonies after we presented these studies on the fruit of the Spirit in various retreats:

> The perfume and fragrance of love has permeated this place. I'm going back to my office with a changed character, and I will practice a quiet heart and tongue.

> I have learned more about God's love and His working in my life. I have five children. I'm going home to turn my home upside down, to change my attitudes and way of being, to pour love into sour situations.

6

My husband is in prison, and I am raising our children alone. I'm determined to love those who have wronged us and change my own attitude.

The curtain has been removed from my mind. I'm going out from here to live Christ and help others.

As the Holy Spirit moved on the hearts of the women during a retreat one evening, there was a period of weeping and heart searching. Maria stood to say: "I didn't want to come here. My heart was rebellious. It was too hot, too rainy, too uncomfortable. Why should I leave my home, come on a bus, be crowded with all those women, sleep on a pallet? But here at the altar the Holy Spirit met me, entered my thought patterns, and rearranged my priorities. I'm going home transformed to live before my husband and neighbors what God is teaching me through the Holy Spirit."

The proof of the pudding is in the eating. The Word transforms—this is what we want.

I will share a word The Holy Spirit gave me while facing deep personal problems in 1955:

"If we are in His will—
We will bear fruit—
God will accomplish
    His will through us.
    We don't have to back down nor give up.
Christ is with us;
The Holy Spirit is within us.
His Word is ours to believe.
God will work *in* us first
Then *through* us to finish His work
    That He gave us to do.
        Face the future
        For God will be with you."

That is what this study is all about. Read, study, change, bear fruit, then go out to live before your world as women transformed—women of grace.

Let the beauty of Jesus be seen in me,
All His wonderful passion and purity,
Oh, sweet Spirit divine, all my nature refine,
Till the beauty of Jesus be seen in me.

How to Use This Book

1. Keep your own personal Bible handy.
2. Have a notebook the same size as this book and a pencil.
3. Look up the Scripture references. This is not an exhaustive study. God will speak to you as you read and study. He will give *you* ideas as to how He wants you to grow.
4. Start a file. As you read *Woman's Touch* magazine, the *Pentecostal Evangel,* Sunday school papers, etc., cut out articles and keep them in categories. Growth isn't accomplished in "10 easy chapters." This is for life; continue to grow in God.
5. Use other versions of the Bible for comparison.
6. Have some simple objects to illustrate each lesson's ideas. (We suggest some.) They don't have to be elaborate, but even adults learn more through the "eye gate."
7. You will find some lists and some little self-exams. Answer the questions, either in your book or in your notebook.
8. For each lesson make a page with the heading: "Questions I Want to Ask When We Meet."
   (This way you won't forget the questions that occurred to you in your personal study when the group meets.)

CHAPTER ONE

How Does Your Garden Grow?

Fruit or Failure

What kind of woman are you? God has a special reason for including minute details of the personal lives of many different women in the Bible. There is a long list of women in the Word, including: Eve, our first mother; Sarah, the mother of a great nation; Rebekah; Rachel; Jochebed; Miriam; Rahab; Ruth; Hannah; Mary; Dorcas; Priscilla; and Tryphena and Tryphosa, the twins who were friends of that great deaconess of the church, Phoebe.

In the lives of these women in the Bible we find some of our own problems; a reflection of contemporary situations. We read about their anger, their complexes, their dilemmas, their rebellion, their reactions, their weaknesses, and their strengths. We read about their families, children, husbands, homes, work, worries, joys, and sorrows. Some were haughty, some were meek; some were dependable, others deceitful. There must be a reason why God included such a complete picture of these women; the complexity and characteristics of their personalities.

I have heard women say, "If I could only have lived during the actual Bible days, I could be a better person, I could be more like Christ." But today we have the Holy Spirit to help us. As we look from our vantage point of these days when God is pouring out His Spirit on all flesh, it is important to see that the Holy Spirit includes women in the fulfillment of the Old Testament prophecy of Joel, as we read in Acts 2:17, 18:

—your sons and daughters shall prophesy
—on my handmaidens I will pour out my Spirit
—they shall prophesy

In our days women are being chosen of God, receiving the infilling of the Holy Spirit, and serving God all over the world. In Latin America, Africa, Asia, Australia, Europe, and every U.S. city, women are being prepared as God's handmaidens. Through the work of the Spirit in our lives and the growth of the fruit within us, He can use us as He used our counterparts, the women in the Word.

We need to learn how to grow more like Christ; how to manifest more of His character and person. By studying the experiences and lives of different women in the Bible we will find help for our own lives, problems, and decisions.

How Does Your Garden Grow?

Our life is like a garden. God wants us to bear fruit. To do this we must make a conscious effort to keep the weeds out and to stay connected to the vine which gives us life.

In this study, we will take the essence of each fruit of the Spirit and discuss how one woman in the Bible manifested this fruit in her life. This will show us how to grow and have the fruit of the Spirit in our lives.

1. Can you identify each of the Bible women in the list at the beginning of this chapter?
2. Do you know something about their problems?

10

3. In what ways might you be like each one?
4. The fruit of the Spirit is listed in Galatians 5:22,
   23. How many of the nine can you name?
5. How many do you feel are growing in your life?

Try to secure several different versions of the Bible.
If you are studying in a group, have members com-
pare them.

Here is a comparison of the words used for the
fruit of the Spirit (Galatians 5:22, 23) in the King
James Version and J. B. Phillips' translation, *The
New Testament in Modern English:*

King James Version	Phillips
1. Love	Love
2. Joy	Joy
3. Peace	Peace
4. Long-suffering	Patience
5. Gentleness	Kindness
6. Goodness	Generosity
7. Faith	Fidelity
8. Meekness	Tolerance
9. Temperance	Self-control

Note: When giving these studies, I write the references from the lesson on slips of paper and give them
to different women before the class begins. Then they
are ready to read the portions without losing time.

Recipe for the Fruitful Life

J. B. Phillips makes Galatians 5:16-23 so under-
standable in *The New Testament in Modern English:*

Here is my advice. Live your whole life in the Spirit
and you will not satisfy the desires of your lower nature.
For the whole energy of the lower nature is set against

11

the Spirit, while the whole power of the Spirit is contrary to the lower nature. Here is the conflict, and that is why you are not free to do what you want to do. But if you follow the leading of the Spirit, you stand clear of the Law.

The activities of the lower nature are obvious. Here is a list: sexual immorality, impurity of mind, sensuality, worship of false Gods, witchcraft, hatred, quarreling, jealousy, bad temper, rivalry, factions, party spirit, envy, drunkenness, orgies and things like that. I solemnly assure you, as I did before, that those who indulge in such things will never inherit God's kingdom. The Spirit, however, produces in human life fruits such as these: love, joy, peace, patience, kindness, generosity, fidelity, tolerance and self-control—and no law exists against any of them.

If our lives are centered in the Spirit, let us be guided by the Spirit.

The Word uses two figures here, that of *walking,* which is the natural growth expression in a child, and that of *growing fruit,* which is the natural expression of a garden. Green vines and leaves are beautiful to look at, but it is fruit that has sweetness, sustenance, and seeds for reproduction. Let us determine to bear fruit in our garden.

Fruit and Gifts

As Pentecostal people we are aware of the moving of the Holy Spirit and know that our distinctive testimony is the infilling of the Holy Spirit, which opens the door to the gifts listed in 1 Corinthians 12 and 14. We hear the word *charismatic* used quite openly these days. On TV, in newspapers, and even in *Time* magazine we find articles about the charismatic outpouring. Actually, of equal importance is the quiet operation of the Holy Spirit in producing fruit in our daily Christian lives.

There must be a balance between the gifts and fruit in our lives. It is interesting to notice there are nine fruit and nine gifts. Both are divine; both are supernatural. They come from divine life; they're not synthetic. Spirituality is not a  quality that you can rub on, then wash off, or put on and take off. It is fruit growing in our lives by a continuous process.

A balance sheet for fruit and gifts might look like this:

Fruit	**Gifts**
Inward for character	Outward for ministry
Being	Doing
Behavior	Believing
Practice	Preach
Takes time	Bestowed immediately
Grows—matures	Perfect at acceptance

Prerequisites to Bearing Fruit

1. Regeneration
   Matthew 7:16-20. A tree must be healthy from its roots.
2. Union with Christ by the Spirit
   John 15:1-8. He is the Vine; we grow from Him, for we are the branches. We must abide in the Vine to grow and bring forth fruit.
3. A desire to walk in the Spirit
   Galatians 5:16-25. We are not robots.
4. Recognition of the law of sowing and reaping
   Galatians 6:7, 8. Here it would be helpful for the group leader to show a potato, an ear of

corn, and a fruit to illustrate the lesson that the kind of seed we plant is what will be produced and will bear fruit.

Contrast Between Fruit and Flesh

Read Galatians 5:19-21 and Colossians 3:5-9. Before we study each of the fruit of the Spirit in detail, let's take a look at where the Holy Spirit begins His work in us. The Scripture passages we just read mention the different activities or inclinations of the lower nature—the weeds in our garden. In checking both these references, I found 24 terms describing the war in our nature.

This means that the work of our own carnal, natural, pre-Christian nature has a broad base. There is more dark than light in our nature. The list includes more than twice as many works of the flesh as fruit of the Spirit. This could be likened to a black velvet jeweler's display cloth. God wants us to realize how brightly His fruit shines, so He puts it against a backdrop of great darkness to show the contrast.

When we look at this list we say, "No, I have no problem with illicit sex, orgies, or drunkenness." But look at that list again. It contains hatred, envy, jealousy, quarreling, rivalry, bad temper, factions. If we honestly check our lives against this list, what do we see? Galatians 5:15 asks, "Do you bite each other? You'll eat each other up." Are you catty? Do you make little snide remarks? This shows a basic insecurity within our own nature. We have to cut at someone else.

Are you jealous? Can you stand it when someone else gets the promotion you wanted? Or, are you busy keeping up with the Joneses? Do you remember that last quarrel when your bad temper flared up? You wished later you hadn't said all those mean things, but they were out, like the feathers out of a pillow shaken in the wind. There is no way to recover them and stuff them back in.

It looks like we need to ask God for the fruit of the Spirit, for His Word says those who *indulge* in the darkness of the lower nature will never inherit God's kingdom. That's terribly clear isn't it? *Indulge*—that's a strong word. That means allowing the weeds to grow, fertilizing them.

Quarreling?

I was playing the piano for an evening prayer meeting once when I heard a commotion at the door of the church. There were two Christians shouting at each other! Finally one struck the other and grabbed some keys out of his hand. One left with his head down. The other took part in the evening service. My heart felt like stone, for I had heard the sound of brass cymbals (1 Corinthians 13).

Going home from a service once, I saw the teacher of the adult women's class get into the car in a huff. Someone had disturbed her. Her daughter asked a question about what they were having for dinner. *Whack!* She hit her across the mouth—that was the only answer she received.

There was a very active person in a certain church who was known to move from house to house without paying her rent or her grocery bills. These situations may be found in your church. The problem is a lack of fruit bearing. We need to become Word-living, fruit-bearing Christians. If we abide in the Vine, the life of Christ will be visible in us.

Pruning Hurts—and Helps!

What does the gardener do as he walks around to check the garden? He takes the pruning shears and cuts. Snip, snip, snip. All the dead parts, all the parts that won't bear fruit, all the parts that are diseased fall away. Sometimes the piles of prunings are higher than the bushes that are left.

Have you ever looked at a rose bush after a master gardener has pruned it? Or, have you lived where they prune grape vines? It makes you wince as they cut them back unmercifully, leaving them so bare, until you wonder if life will ever come again. Ah, the gardener knows what he's doing. Careful pruning lets the life flow and create fruit.

(Take pruning shears and clip a branch off to show the class. If you leave it out awhile it will become completely dried with no life in it. If we don't remain in the Vine we will dry up and our leaves and fruit will fall off. We will be useless.)

Witchcraft. You say this isn't a pagan country. There's no witchcraft? What about that horoscope column in every popular magazine? Do you allow your actions to be influenced by it? This is contrary to God's plan. It is part of the darkness; part of the weeds.

Dirty language and lies. Do you laugh at off-color jokes? Or, does your presence sanctify your office or place of work? Do your companions know your word is honest and true? I like what President Eisenhower once said: "I always tell the truth, then I don't have to remember what I've said."

Rivalry, jealousy, factions, even party spirit, warring, and fighting. These too are works of the flesh, growing in untended gardens, neglected vineyards, lives of severed relationships with the Vine.

It may be that all of us will feel as if the Master Gardener has walked through our garden and done a lot of clipping during these studies. Perhaps He will convict us of sin and create a climate for real growth within us!

Activities of the lower nature that cause conflict and keep us stunted in our growth include:

Galatians 5:19-21	**Colossians 3:5-11**
adultery	shameful desires
sexual impurity	worshiping the good things
impurity of mind	of life
sensuality	anger
worshiping false	hatred
gods	cursing
witchcraft	dirty language
hatred	lying
quarreling	holding grudges
jealousy	race bigotry
bad temper	
rivalry	
factions	
party spirit	
envy	
drunkenness	
orgies	
other things like that—	

Below is a list of women all of us know—do you find yourself? Let's try to change each name to a positive one.

Agnes Angry	Agnes Agreeable
Bertha Blunt	Bertha ?
Cathy Cat	_____
Derva Don't	_____
Emma Empty	_____
Flossie Flirt	_____
Gail Gripe	_____
Hilda Hurry	_____
Iva Irritable	_____
Jill Jumpy	_____

Karen Krank _____
Liza Lazy _____
Martha Magpie _____
Nellie Nag _____
Olga Odor _____
Patty Pout _____
Queenie Querulous _____
Ruth Rampage _____
Sally Sour _____
Tilly Tantrum _____
Eunice Upset _____
Vera Vixen _____
Wendy Wicked _____
Ynga Yell _____
Zeta Zany _____

Check Your Garden of Attitudes

Put an *X* in pencil under the appropriate space.

Do You . . .

	Rarely	Some-times	Often
1. Shout at your husband?	____	____	____
2. Gripe about your neighbor?	____	____	____
3. Yell at your kids?	____	____	____
4. Open your child's mail?	____	____	____
5. Criticize his friends?	____	____	____
6. Cut down his teachers?	____	____	____
7. Lose your cool when hot?	____	____	____
8. Yank at your child?	____	____	____

9. Criticize your pastor?   —— —— ——
10. Wear dirty clothes around?   —— —— ——
11. Whine?   —— —— ——
12. Demand your rights?   —— —— ——
13. Visit sick friends?   —— —— ——
14. Thank your children for helping?   —— —— ——
15. Fix flowers in your home?   —— —— ——
16. Praise your husband?   —— —— ——
17. Respect your pastor?   —— —— ——
18. Welcome your child with love?   —— —— ——
19. Show affection at home?   —— —— ——
20. Speak quietly?   —— —— ——
21. Smile at sales people?   —— —— ——

Be Big Enough

Be big enough to live the life God gave you,
Untouched by petty selfishness and greed—
Stand free from foolish habits which enslave you,
Be big enough to meet your greatest need.

Be big enough to speak the truth—and live it,
Hold your ideals though the heavens fall—
Expect no quarter, yet be quick to give it—
Be big enough to heed the humblest call.

Be big enough to smile, when all about you,
Your very world lies crumbled in the dust—
Have courage to fight on when your friends doubt you,

Be big enough to keep your faith and trust.

Be big enough that changing years may find you,
Regretting not the ones you've left behind—
Be quick to throw off prejudice which binds you,
Be big enough to keep an open mind.

Be big enough to say—I was mistaken,
Be slow to take offense, quick to forgive—
Let pity, justice, love—in your heart waken,
Be big enough, and kind enough, to live.

—Anonymous

CHAPTER TWO

Love

Mary, The Poured Out Life

MARK 14:3-9 & JOHN 12:1-9

Mary peeked through the door and saw all the disciples sitting there at the table along with her brother Lazarus. Just a few days ago they had buried him and she and Martha had wondered how they were going to get along. The two sisters were alone in the house and their hearts full of grief.

And there sat Jesus. He was the One who had said, "Lazarus, come forth." Ah, He had told her so many things when she sat at His feet while her older sister Martha was busy getting dinner.

Suddenly she knew she had to do something. Her heart was bursting with love and gratitude. "The fruit of the Spirit is love. . . ." Words were hollow. How could she say thanks?

She brought the most costly thing of her life. She didn't own any jewels or have a bank account, savings, or bonds. But every week she had put a bit of ointment into that perfume jar. It was reserved for her burial. Since she was a single woman, she had to look ahead and provide for her own burial.

She Forgot Herself

She slipped in through the door and broke the top off the alabaster bottle. She didn't measure the contents—drop, drop, drop. She poured every drop of that expensive nard perfume all over the feet of Jesus, then wiped His feet with her hair. She forgot herself and others.

"Oh, what a waste!" snarled Judas. He was the treasurer and his quick mind immediately calculated that she had spilled perfume worth the amount of a man's salary for a full year. "That's worth a fortune! We could have helped the orphanage. We could have given it to missions! We could have built an addition on the church. Oh, what a waste!"

Poured Out

There wasn't any way to scoop up even a little. It was all poured out. She hadn't reserved a drop for herself. It was impulsive abandonment. It was reckless. It was a foolish, sentimental gesture.

Jesus Understands

Then came the words of the Master. "Let her alone, she has done what she could. She has done a good work." I've needed that word at times. Don't we all?

As a woman she had given what was hers—her life's savings. It belonged to her. Maybe it seemed like a rash, impulsive action, but the gift was hers to give. Jesus doesn't expect of us more than we can do; He understands.

"You will always have the poor, and the needy, but you won't always have me." Yes, there will be projects, social work, and the poor always. And there will always be someone to criticize—someone to calculate, to cut you down, to say you should have done it differently. Rejection can create bitterness when you've done your best. Unjust criticism hardens the most spontaneous heart.

Keep Your Motive Pure

Here's where fruit bearing pays off. Your motive must be love. Keep your eyes on Jesus. Obey the nudging of the Spirit.

"She has anointed my body for the burial." What a strange thing to say. "But you are eating at this table in perfect health. Only a few days ago you raised Lazarus from the dead. You said, 'I am the way, the truth and the life.' What does this mean?" Only Jesus and the Father knew that within 6 days He would go to the cross to give His life.

We understand now. We see from this side of Calvary. Let's not be too hard on the 12 men who walked with Him, ate with Him, and learned from Him. They couldn't see the whole picture.

Mary, the sensitive woman of grace, had the spiritual perception to minister to Him. She could have thought some other time would be more appropriate, and waited. But it was God's plan for the heart of a woman to obey His prompting to prepare her Lord in advance for the cross.

A Memorial to Mary

"Wherever this gospel is preached, she will be remembered, because she gave and poured out this perfume." It will be a memorial of her.

I can almost smell the fragrance of that perfume now as I write here in my kitchen. It seems filled with the presence of that ointment. In Bolivia I smelled it when I saw Indian women visiting the hospitals and walking miles to tell others about Christ. In Argentina I sensed the fragrance as a Jewish convert, Beba, working as a cosmetologist over the faces of TV stars, brought Christ to them in their need.

In Africa and in Germany there is that same fragrance. What is it? It's love. The fragrance of love is wafted down across every century. Today I sensed the fragrance when I saw my 58-year-old friend get down on her hands and knees to show two little abandoned boys how to play with clay. There was an odor of stale cat food in the room. Their mother was in jail on a drugs charge. But I detected the fragrance of love working right there in a needy area. It was fresh and pungent and all other odors were unnoticed. That fragrance can linger in your home too.

The Law of Love

Mary is remembered wherever the gospel is preached in all the world. This tender woman is remembered because she poured out all she possessed in love on our Lord. This is the law of love. You can give without loving, but you can't love without giving.

I remember when my 4-year-old Rachel climbed out onto a balcony to reach over to pick a little yellow Scotch Broom (almost the only flower that grew readily at 13,000 feet above sea level). You think it's a weed? Yes, but she brought it with the love of her heart for my birthday. We put it in a vase.

The same day a jeweler friend of our family gave me a large aquamarine knowing it was my birthstone. Later he offered to mount it in a ring for me. I trustingly returned it to him. It was worth a great deal, but he never gave it back. The fragrance of Rachel's flower is sweeter.

You Can't Hoard Love

Love holds no reserves. "Why this waste?" was the criticism 26 years ago when we prepared ourselves to go as young missionaries to the heart of South America. Professional members of our family said, "Why are you going to waste your lives?"

You can't save love; you can't hoard it. For love to

grow you must give it away. My heart sings:

All for Jesus, all for Jesus
All my days and all my hours—
All for Jesus, all for Jesus,
All my being's ransomed powers.

A Hymn of Love

I would like to share Paul's hymn of love, the great love chapter—1 Corinthians 13—with you from various versions. I feel the purity of the Word applied to our lives here is like the carpenter's level or the jeweler's magnifying glass that penetrates to check the real intrinsic value.

This love chapter is sandwiched in between chapters 12 and 14 which give the instructions for the operation of the gifts of the Spirit in our lives and the church.

Read together 1 Corinthians 13 from the King James Version. Verse 1 says if we speak with tongues in church and our testimony isn't motivated by love, no one will listen for it will be a false testimony. It will fall flat. Verses 2 and 3 remind us that even great works and miracles and all our charitable philanthropic works arc hollow without love. Now let's share verses 4-7 together directly from the Word from three different versions:

The Living Bible

Love is very patient and kind,
Never jealous or envious,
Never boastful or proud,
Never haughty or selfish or rude.
Love does not demand its own way.
It is not irritable or touchy,
It does not hold grudges
And will hardly even notice when others do it wrong.
It is never glad about injustice,

But rejoices whenever truth wins out.
If you love someone you will be loyal to him no matter what the cost.
You will always believe in him,
Always expect the best of him,
And always stand your ground in defending him.

Phillips

This love of which I speak is slow to lose patience—it looks for a way of being constructive.
It is not possessive:
It is neither anxious to impress
Nor does it cherish inflated ideas of its own importance.
Love has good manners and does not pursue selfish advantage.
It is not touchy.
It does not keep account of evil or gloat over the wickedness of other people.
On the contrary, it is glad with all good men when truth prevails.
Love knows no limit to its endurance,
No end to its trust, no fading of its hope;
It can outlast anything.
It is, in fact, the one thing that still stands when all else has fallen.

New English Bible

Love is patient; love is kind and envies no one.
Love is never boastful, nor conceited, nor rude;
Never selfish, not quick to take offense.
Love keeps no score of wrongs;
Does not gloat over other men's sins, but delights in the truth.
There is nothing love cannot face;

There is no limit to its faith, its hope, and its endurance.

Touchy

Do you like to be around touchy people? The Word says love is "not quick to take offense." I remember the day my gentle husband said to me, "Honey, I see you're growing in God. I saw you be quiet. Not so quick to fly to your own defense; you are learning to do good to those who despitefully use you." It made my heart happy, but at the same time it was a gentle reminder that it had been obvious before that I was quick to exonerate myself. I want to keep growing in God's grace.

Courteous

Love is kind, gentle, patient, and courteous. If we are courteous in our homes to our husband and children, they will respond in the same manner. Love is constructive. Instead of cutting someone down, try to think of how you can lift him up.

Love costs us. Can we find the positive side in difficult situations? If your children come dashing in with muddy feet on a freshly waxed floor, control yourself. Be glad they are alive and able to run.

No Score of Wrongs

Love doesn't keep a "little black book," a score of wrongs. In the musical drama *"I Do, I Do,"* which is the story of 50 years of married life, there is a typical scene between the husband and wife. He says, "I must inform you I have made a little list of all your irritating habits." "Really," the wife answers, "I have also taken the liberty to make a little list," and she pulls a list about 7 feet long out of a drawer!

"The first is, you chew in your sleep, *Zzzzcch, Zzzzch!*"

"How awful."

"Yes, I quite agree."

It's really amusing, as it shows how we let little irritations dim our love. We concentrate on making lists. We make mountains out of molehills and suddenly our love is clouded over. Love doesn't insist on "my rights."

Quit Nagging

I once heard a woman tell how she would find Scripture passages to "hit her husband over the head with." They just fit. She gloated over how she could hit him scripturally with all his faults. Then someone asked, "Do you want to live alone? Quit nagging!"

Love is kind. Have you heard someone whip another in public prayer? Love finds a better way to communicate—one that builds up instead of cutting down.

It Seems Impossible

During my last 6 months in Argentina, I went each week to the home of Pilar, an agnostic philosophy teacher who had cancer. I had started to testify to her 5 years before when her heart was closed. Now she was realizing her need. We would read, chat, and pray together.

The third week when I came back Pilar said: "Oh, you left that portion in 1 John 4 with me. I had decided that I wanted to find the love of God. I think I'm ready to be His. But I read all that chapter and it troubled me so I couldn't sleep. This says that to love God I must also love those around me. That is impossible, Betty Jane. There are those who have wronged me. I would rather get even with them. The Bible says

28

they'll know we are disciples if we have love one for another. I see this very clearly. I must be ready to love others, if I would love God, but how can I?"

This was real candor. The Word was cutting into her darkened mind. Yes, humanly speaking love is not a natural function. We would rather get even with someone who has wronged us. In the soil of love the other fruit grow. A woman said to me, "Oh, sure I love everyone, but I'm choosy about who I like!"

Love is the sum of all the graces, the healer of memories, the royal law of the Scriptures. The beauty of the fruit of the Spirit is that it's like a bunch of grapes. There are many parts, but all one fruit. Look at a beautiful bunch of grapes, each part lovely, succulent, and perfect. Thus, in love we find patience, kindness, meekness, gentleness, goodness, self-control, faith—all parts, but a whole.

Love Endures

When everything is gone; when the house we spent lots of time on has been torn down, when the pictures we painted have been auctioned off, when the cakes we baked are eaten, when the sweaters we knitted are full of moth holes, when the bandages we rolled are burned, what will still last? It will be the memory—the reality of love. They will remember, "there was a fragrance in her life. She was kind and she loved me." Love endures.

Questions for Personal Answers

1. Why does Mary typify the fruit "love"?
2. How does John 3:16 show us what the law of love is?
3. What does Romans 5:8 tell us about love?
4. What does it teach us about our love toward others?

5. First John 4:7, 8 shows us the source of love which can grow and rule our lives. What is it?
6. Does this mean we are like God?
7. Do you have Pilar's problem with 1 John 4:20, 21?
8. What kind of relationship should you have with someone you love according to 1 John 4:18?
9. Do you feel your heart becoming tender?
10. Have you misjudged someone? How can you heal and rectify it?
11. Have you had a misunderstanding in your home? How can you remedy it?
12. How important is it for you to keep Ephesians 4:32 as the law of your home?
13. Make a list of the good things about yourself. ("I have to live with myself and so I want to be fit for myself to know.")
14. Whom do you love most?
15. What makes you love him/her?
16. Whom do you have trouble liking?
17. Why do they grate on you?
18. Are they different?
19. How can you change your enemies into friends?
20. How can you express your love and gratitude?
21. How can we forget the wrongs we've suffered?
22. Since love is the rule of your life, make a list of the people you would like to help by showing God's love.

CHAPTER THREE

Joy

Two Pregnant Women
Mary and Elisabeth

LUKE 1:35-55

Do you remember the story of the little boy who visited his grandmother's farm one Sunday? The lamb came scampering, jumping for joy. The dog jumped and wagged his tail. "Down, Rover, it's Sunday, you mustn't jump around," he said. Then he saw the mule standing with his ears down, his eyes sad, and his head bowed, "Ah, my grandma would say you're the only real Christian on this farm!"

Does being a Christian mean no joy? Does it mean you can't have a good time? Do you let a problem throw you? sour you? Are you dragging your feet with the humidity? In a line at the supermarket which faces reflect joy? What about your own?

A Sad Heart Tires in a Mile

Proverbs 17:22 says that a joyful heart is as good as a medicine, but a broken spirit makes one sick. Do you know the truth in this? Joy can be the antidote for what is ailing our world, our churches, and our own personal lives.

"The fruit of the Spirit is . . . joy." Joy is a natural result of our salvation, the outward manifestation of inner well-being. We've visited many homes while traveling among churches on our furloughs. We find homes where there is a dullness, a sour attitude.

31

The joy is gone. The family still goes to church and may even pay their tithes, but there is no buoyancy, no joy. A joyful heart makes a light step; joy increases our efficiency. Think about your own life; have you gone sour?

Elisabeth the Barren

Let's go to the Word to read about two women of grace who kept their joy in a difficult situation. As we read Luke 1:35-55, we find these two important women. The first is an older woman who had been childless all her life, ministering in the temple with her priest-husband. Suddenly at 70 years of age Elisabeth found she was pregnant.

This would lift the pressure of bearing the stigma of being a barren Jewish wife, but how would she have the strength to bear a child when her body was no longer young? How would this affect her ministry with her husband? How would she be able to care for a tiny baby?

Mary, the Virgin

On the other hand, we find a beautiful, young single girl, well thought of in the village. She had always gone with the other girls to draw water from the well. Now her body was beginning to swell with a pregnancy. The mothers shook their heads and warned their daughters, "Don't you have anything to do with Mary. She got herself into trouble."

She was misunderstood, frowned upon, and maligned. Even her family felt the social pressure. There was the possibility of a broken engagement. The Jewish laws said Joseph must take her out and stone her to death. She couldn't be sure he would understand and believe the angel had really spoken to her.

There was reproach all around her. The old women

spoke behind their hands; the young girls avoided her. Moral suffering and being misunderstood are much more traumatic than physical punishment. They affect our inner nature and can put out the fire of our joy. Pregnant at 70 or at 17—both could bring problems.

How Do We Wait?

We read that Elisabeth waited for the birth of her son John. I believe she was praying for this person who was being formed within her. She surrounded him with positive thoughts. God was preparing the evangelist who would be the forerunner of our Lord. After 6 months Mary walked to the mountain village to visit her cousin. The moment Mary knocked and called, "Hello, how's everyone?" Elisabeth said, "Oh, I felt life; my baby leaped for joy!"

The Miracle of Birth

When we feel those movements of a baby as our body swells out of proportion, and he kicks us under one rib and stretches an arm down into our pelvic area, we are uncomfortable. We can't lie in any position to sleep, for the baby moves around. There are those early days of nausea when everything flips upside down. We could allow antagonism and dread to replace our joy. "It hurts. Look at the stretch marks. This will disfigure me for life. I'm losing my muscle tone!"

If we read Psalm 139:1-18 it will help us to see the miracle of birth. God knows about that baby. God surrounds you with His care from the day of conception. Think of the great miracle as the baby grows, the arms and legs move, the fingernails take shape. At conception there is the fusion of two cells. This miracle of fusion results in millions of possible combinations of characteristics.

We are part of God's miracle, for our attitude as women bearing children can be joy through all 9 months of waiting.

Abortion?

Rather than toying with the thought that is so prevalent today, "If I don't want this baby, I don't have to carry him," both Mary and Elisabeth rejoiced in God. Let us as Christian women teach our daughters and also accept in ourselves the reality of God's joy for these waiting days. Between 1970 and 1977 there were more than 5 million abortions in the United States. As Christians we need to emphasize the value of life and the joy of being a part of God's miracle in giving life.

The Song

Mary's beautiful answer to Elisabeth's joy was to break forth into singing (Luke 1:47-55). This portion of Scripture is known as the Magnificat. She sang out: "My soul magnifies God; my heart is overflowing. I will praise my Lord. My spirit is full of joy in God my Saviour."

Mary kept her heart singing in spite of outward obstacles. Could you or I have kept our heads lifted, our spirits right, and joy in our hearts? Yes, if we were living in the Spirit and the fruit of joy was growing in our lives!

Tidings of Great Joy

No wonder the announcement of the angels in Luke 2:10 came with great joy.

Joy to the world, the Lord is come!
Let earth receive her King.

*   *   *   *   *

Oh sing with joy, sing with joy,
Joy, joy, joy, joy, joy, joy,
Joy to the Lord who reigns on high.

The most heavenly message the angels could bring was: "We bring news of great joy, unto you is born this day, a Saviour who will bring to all nations, to all the world, to all peoples, joy."

We have seen the transformation on the faces of those who walked in great darkness when they heard the news and accepted Christ as Saviour. Their eyes shone, their mouth relaxed; joy filled and completely transformed them.

I remember walking one Christmas Eve to the different plazas of La Paz, Bolivia to sing with our choir. At my side walked several young people. Rosario, a new Christian said, "I don't know why I waited, for since I walked to the altar and opened my life to Jesus I have such joy."

There is no joy in paganism, whether in a so-called Christian nation or in a heathen country. People may beat their drums and dance and sing, but their hearts are hollow. Jesus brings joy.

What Does Joy Mean for Us Today?

1. Joy is our Christian *privilege* and the best advertisement for the gospel
   a. John 15:11—have fullness of joy
   b. John 16:22—no one can take away your joy
   c. 1 Thessalonians 1:6—joy in the Holy Spirit
   d. James 1:2, 3—joy in problems
2. Joy is our *strength*
   a. Nehemiah 8:10—joy of the Lord is our strength
   b. Habakkuk 3:17-18—in spite of circumstances

35

3. Joy is our *medicine*
   a. Proverbs 17:22—good for what ails us
   b. Isaiah 61:1-3—replaces sorrow
4. Joy makes us really *fulfilled*
   a. Psalm 16:11—fullness of joy
   b. 1 Peter 1:8—creates rejoicing
5. Joy is *contagious*
   a. Acts 8:8—they wanted to buy it
   b. John 4:39—they saw the Samaritan woman changed
   c. Psalm 51:12—restore our joy so we can minister to others

Well-being

These Scripture passages help us to realize that real joy is not the froth of merriment that comes with revelry. The joy of the Lord is the abiding sense of well-being. Despondency is not for the Christian. Job 20:5 tells us that the joy of a hypocrite doesn't last. Television programs are filled with laughter without joy. They are artificial.

I like the thought from Proverbs 17:22 that joy is a medicine. Having joy keeps the spirit from drying up. When my 82-year-old father had a stroke, my sister wrote that although the thrombosis had caused near blindness, he would wait for them at the hospital door. When he identified a voice, he always had a joke or some light-hearted banter to keep the spirit alive.

There are books written on E.I.I. (emotionally induced illness). Some doctors affirm that 85 percent of contemporary illness is induced by the emotions. The feeling of insecurity, the lack of confidence, actually create real sickness. How much of it could be cured with a real injection of joy? Pills and prescriptions will never cure the sour spirit. The fruit of the Spirit is joy.

Joy in Place of Mourning

One of the first things that made us curious in South America was the sight of so many people dressed in black. Many men wore black arm bands on their new suits. When we inquired about it we found it indicated mourning. If a mother or wife died the man wore black for 7 years, and then the black arm band indefinitely. If the deceased was not a close relative, the black was worn for 3 to 5 years.

As we searched the Scriptures, Isaiah 61:1-3 became very real to us. The preaching of the gospel is for the brokenhearted, the captives, and those who mourn. Jesus says He will give beauty for ashes. He gives the oil of joy for mourning and the garment of praise for the spirit of heaviness. In place of sorrow and nervous tension, Jesus brings joy. He trades us joy for sorrow and a robe of praise for the old gunnysack of heaviness. As women we need this trade. This trade is wisdom—it's good business! We can't lose. He offers to trade us "even" and we come out ahead. This is the way He planned it.

Sorrow takes its toll on the face, the figure, and the attitude. But Jesus says, "Come, I will trade you, I will give you joy."

One day before my mother died she said, "I am not afraid. To die is to go to sleep and wake up in the presence of Jesus." She did just that—took my father's hand and went to sleep. Without a sigh or groan, she was with Jesus.

Dying is not a complicated matter for the Christian. Jesus will be with us in time of death to bring that sweet abiding joy and inner well-being. He is with the one who goes to be with Him, and He is also with us who remain so that we sorrow not as those who have no hope.

37

Contagious

Just as we've shown that joy is contagious, failure and sorrow are also contagious. We are transparent. Our life and attitude as women affects the tone of our home and our husband and children. If we are bitter, always ready with a sharp cutting word, they will begin to wither. We can wield death with a sharp glance.

Have you watched a dog put his tail between his legs and slink away? He may have come wagging his tail with such joy, and then we scolded. The lack of joy in our life bears the same fruit in our home. Try modulating your voice to include joy and buoyancy. Your children will quit whining too.

Dragging?

Are your feet heavy? You just can't get around to pushing the vacuum, making the beds, setting a nice table? Try putting on some soft Christian music. Sing along with your favorite singer. Lift your heart toward your Lord as Mary did:

> *Magnify the Lord with me,*
> *Blessed Lamb of Calvary.*
> *For His grace so full and free,*
> *Oh, magnify the Lord with me.*

As joy permeates your soul, your strength will be renewed, the broom will feel lighter, the potatoes will get peeled, and suddenly you'll realize the work is all finished—kitchen cleaned, dusting done, beds made. The joy of the Lord is your strength!

Sometimes we get weary in well-doing. Busy with baking cookies for VBS, helping at the women's meetings, getting our children's clothes ready for camp, preparing uniforms for the Missionettes group and clothes for Royal Rangers—busy, busy, busy. When you feel your shoulders droop, your eyes go hollow, your mouth become drawn, set your heart and mind on Jesus and begin to sing. We must have a real desire for the growth of joy in our lives.

Try changing your attitude. Try to think of a positive compliment to meet your son with, "I really appreciate your taking out the garbage," or, "Thanks for bringing in the groceries." Instead of screaming, "Your room is always a mess. Socks in the corners, jeans under the bed, I get so tired!" No wonder he retreats to the TV!

Now this is going to take some work. We fall into a rut of saying the first sour thing we think of. Try changing your tactics and your joy will catch fire.

Wonderful, wonderful Jesus,
In my heart He implanteth a song,
A song of deliverance, of courage and strength,
In my heart He implanteth a song.

There is never a day so dreary,
There is never a night so long
But the soul that is trusting in Jesus
Will somewhere find a song.

Rejoicing in Serving

I have a letter from my young pastor son, Rocky, written from Wisconsin in the cold of January. He begins: "Joy to you today! We've been rejoicing a great deal in the Lord these past 3 weeks." (I have that line underlined in red for it blesses my heart.) As he continues he tells about a youth retreat where 88 young people studied the theme "Worship, Sharing Jesus, My Lord, and Knowing and Using Your Gift." Then he says: "It was a tremendous experience for Sherry and me as our two restaurant hotel majors who were going to do the cooking backed out at the last minute. Sherry had to take over in those crowded quarters for all those kids. But it inspired care for one another. She did a fantastic job.''

I realized that Sherry was 8 months pregnant at the time and had been thinking of going to the retreat to study and share. She had to assume all that kitchen work at the last minute. He says they are rejoicing! Isn't that great!

Don't Blow It

I am reminded of a day my husband and I spent with Rocky and Sherry while they were at the Assemblies of God Graduate School in Springfield, Missouri, preparing to go as missionaries. It was Sherry's birthday, so we decided to go out for lunch at a favorite salad buffet.

Sherry was dressed in a lovely, long white linen skirt, but her baby unexpectedly dampened it. On the way to the restaurant we ran out of gas on a back street. We put the hood up and sat there in the 95-percent humidity with the curl coming out of our fresh hairdos, while my husband went to find a gas station. A friendly man picked him up and brought him back with the gas.

After we put the gas in the car we returned to the station to fill up the tank. The attendant carelessly let the hose hang loose and it pressure-sprayed gas all over Rocky's one new suit and filled his shoes, burning his feet. So we stopped at a store to buy some socks and he went into a restroom to wash his feet.

"We're nearly there," Sherry announced. "Watch for the Ford sign near the exit from the highway we need to take. There it is."

"Oops, we've gone by. Well, no sweat," Rocky said. "We'll take the next exit and return."

The exit was further down the highway than we had expected, but we finally turned around, drove back, and—missed it again! But eventually we had our special lunch.

We were late, hot, and hungry, but we kept our cool. Later we agreed that not much more could have happened. Still, there wasn't one word of blame, not even a smirk or lifted eyebrow. It would have been so easy—we could have lost our joy. Then we would have sounded like this:

Why? Why? Why?

"Why did you forget to buy gas? You know the gauge isn't working. You mustn't trust it." "Why did you take that back road where you knew there wouldn't be any traffic?" "Why didn't you start to get ready sooner?" "Why did you go so fast and miss that exit? Why didn't you slow down? Why don't you listen to me? I told you where to turn." "Why are you always coaching me?" "Why did you stand so near that pump?" "Why did we even get up today?"

The whining could have continued all afternoon. We would have blown it. The whole day would have gone sour.

Joy was the medicine for our situation. God helped us to keep happy hearts. We were able to laugh at our problems. A sense of humor coupled with inner joy brings quiet help in difficult circumstances. Actually, it is in a crisis that the character of a person is revealed.

My prayer for you is that the joy of the Lord may be your strength and your medicine and that your joy may be full.

An Encounter With Truth

1. Have you known someone who faced pregnancy

with dread? How can we show the beauty of pregnancy from Psalm 139?

2. Psalm 139:1 says God knew us from our very beginning. Verse 13 says He covered us in our mother's womb; verse 14, that we are wonderfully made. How should we relate this knowledge to the popular feeling about abortion today?

3. What should we teach our young people about the sanctity of life?

4. How do you think Mary's attitude of joy affected Jesus?

5. What is the "fullness of joy" we experience in Christ? Read John 15:11 and Psalm 16:11.

6. How can an attitude of joy help us when we have a lot of work to do?

7. Habakkuk 3:17-19 is one of the loveliest pieces of poetry ever written. What is its message?

8. What are some of the circumstances you face in which you need the fruit of the Spirit which is joy?

9. What did David mean in Psalm 51:12 when he wrote, "Restore my joy"? How had he lost it? When do we need our joy restored?

CHAPTER FOUR

Peace

Jochebed, Woman of Destiny

NUMBERS 26:59,
EXODUS 2:1-11 and 1:15

We are living in a day of pills—pink, green, purple, orange, yellow, large, small. We have a friend who couldn't sleep, so she took a pill. Then she couldn't wake up, so she took a pill to activate her. And she couldn't concentrate, so she took another one. She was like a walking zombie. Today, after many years of this abuse, she is unable to function effectively.

"The fruit of the Spirit is . . . peace." Why do we allow pressures and problems to rob us of our peace? Peace is the natural fruit of the Spirit that begins to grow as soon as we know Christ as our Saviour. God's peace is His antidote for today's problems and fears. Romans 5:1 says: "Since then it is by faith that we are justified, let us grasp the fact that we have peace with God through our Lord Jesus Christ" *(Phillips)*. Our conscience has been cleansed. We begin our Christian growth in an atmosphere of peace.

Peace *With* God or *of* God

This verse in Romans says we have peace *with* God. This is the peace that comes when we are reconciled with God through Christ. Then there is the peace *of* God which is the fruit that grows in our lives. Unfortunately, many who actually are saved and know Christ have peace *with* God, but the peace *of* God isn't growing in their lives.

When Jesus was in the boat during the storm, He laid down and went to sleep. He is the Author of peace, internal peace, and peace in the elements. The disciples had accepted peace *with* God, but they evidently didn't have the peace *of* God for they worried all night. Finally, they accused Jesus of wanting to drown them and not caring about them. Fear had destroyed their peace.

Jesus is our peace. He says, "Lo, I am with you alway."

What are you afraid of?
—noises in the night?
—your son doesn't come home when expected?
—you can't make your money stretch?
—losing your job?
—growing old?
—ridicule, loss of face?

Let's explore together what God says about peace:

1. The Source of Peace
   John 14:27—"Peace I leave with you," not the kind the world gives but a deep abiding peace that is independent of circumstances.
   Job 22:21—"Acquaint now thyself with him and be at peace." Our peace comes from knowing Jesus, the Prince of Peace.

2. Quality of His Peace
   Philippians 4:7—"The peace of God which passeth all understanding, shall keep your hearts and minds through Christ Jesus."

Here is a double-pronged promise: The strength of His peace will keep: our hearts and minds; our emotions and thoughts.

3. Keeping His Peace
   Isaiah 26:3—"Thou wilt keep him in perfect peace, whose mind is stayed on thee: because he trusteth in thee."

1 Peter 5:7—"Casting all your care upon him; for he careth for you."

Colossians 3:15—"Let the peace of God rule in your hearts." We have a volitional part in keeping His peace.

4. Growth in Peace

1 Peter 3:11—"Seek peace and pursue it."

Hebrews 4:1-11—There is a rest that God has provided for the children of God. We must enter into that rest. It is a higher dimension; the calm in the center of a storm.

Philippians 4:8—"Think on these things."

5. Results of His Peace

Proverbs 3:23-26—We can walk, work, live, and sleep without worry for the Lord is our confidence.

Psalm 4:8—"I will both lay me down in peace and sleep; for thou, Lord, only makest me dwell in safety."

We remember the thought of love being the central part of the fruit. But if there is no peace, no fruit can grow. If there are envy, jealousy, clashing spirits, and warring factions, we are stunted. If there is always that feeling of competition it takes away our peace.

What Is Peace?

Peace is tranquility of spirit. Peace is a quiet conscience before God, knowing we have a correct relationship with God. Peace is the absence of war and fear. First John 4:18 says, "There is no fear in love; but perfect love casteth out fear." Fear robs us of peace; lack of peace brings worry and anxiety.

Fear is the most disintegrating factor in the human personality. Thousands of people are destroying their lives because of anxiety, fear, and worry. Yet we are told that 92 percent of all the things we fear will never take place. We cross our bridges before we get to them. How foolish we are to live in fear of tomorrow. God has all our tomorrows in His hand.

We mentioned E.I.I. in the chapter on joy. Many times emotional imbalance is due to fear. Fear creates ulcers and heart problems. It affects our physical, spiritual, and social well-being. Let's find God's antidote in peace, the fruit of the Spirit.

Here is a list of some expressions of fear: anxiety, worry, suspicion, doubts, indecision, hesitancy, timidity, cowardice, inferiority, tension, loneliness, and overaggression.

Can you make a list of some expressions of peace?

Where Do We Need Peace?

We need peace between ourselves and our husbands, among our children, in school, at work, in our mind, and in our nerves. Peace comes from God but it's up to us to accept and keep it.

If there is jealousy, envy, bitterness, and quarreling, peace can't grow. If we are nagging and cantankerous, we have war within us. Even though we may have obtained peace *with* God, we are not maintaining the peace *of* God in our lives.

What we talk about at the table while all the family is present is very important for our physical well-being. Some parents wait to do all their correcting and scolding until the child comes to the table. This atmosphere creates knots in the stomach and a physical imbalance so food doesn't digest well. It can also create a climate of fear that leaves a mark for life.

Up to *Us*

Isaiah 26:3 puts most of the burden for our peace directly on us: "Thou wilt keep him in perfect peace whose mind is stayed on thee, because he trusteth in thee.'' We must keep our minds fixed on God, thinking His thoughts.

In my memory I hear my mother say, "But the peace of God which passeth all understanding will keep your hearts and minds through Christ Jesus" (Philippians 4:7). Here is a double promise. God's peace is so great it is beyond our comprehension. It will keep our hearts (that is, our emotions), our nerves (the feeling part of us), and our minds (our thinking, reasoning capacity; the intelligent part of us).

Verse 8 tells us what we must think about: "Finally, whatsoever things are true, whatsoever things are honest, whatsoever things are just, whatsoever things are pure, whatsoever things are lovely, whatsoever things are of good report; if there be any virtue, and if there be any praise, *think on these things.*"

What do you think about while driving? What do you think about while peeling potatoes? Would you like to have your thoughts put on a screen for your family to see? What influences the way you think? What positive things can we think about?

Colossians 3:15 invites us to "let the peace of God rule [our] hearts."

I believe there is a secret here for women. Many of our problems come from not *letting* God's peace pervade and fill our lives so that it comes in and flows out through us to others.

I remember how my grandmother many years ago loved to listen to *Ma Perkins* on the radio. She laughed, she cried; she identified with that family. Today, TV soap operas are captivating the time, the minds, and the emotions of millions of women. They live vicariously the lives of the TV characters. They often borrow their problems and apply them to their own families. They allow the programs to rob them of peace. Their housework is not finished, the dinner isn't started, and their children are unruly. We need to realize that the TV has an off switch. If we are watching something that undermines our personal peace and doesn't contribute to keeping our hearts and minds fixed on God, it's up to *us* to flip the button.

Anything we do that threatens the peace of our home needs to be changed. It may be a handcraft or a club. It may even be going to church without caring properly for our home and family before we go.

If—If—If

I have a nervous Christian friend who lives in a land of "ifs"—"What if my son gets hurt? What if he's tempted with drugs? What if he's in an accident? What if my husband has financial reverses?" She calls me anxiously to request, "Pray for my son, I'm so worried about him."

She creates a stormy atmosphere with her worry. We are responsible for the presence of peace in our homes. One friend wrote to me after my husband had stayed in their home during a seminar, "Betty Jane, your husband brought an atmosphere of peace into our home, there was the quiet presence of peace around him." This is the fruit of the Spirit in operation.

Learning to "Cast"

First Peter 5:7 doesn't indicate that Christians won't ever have problems. We may have problems, pressures, reverses, and disappointments, but it's how we handle them that shows whether we have peace: "Casting all your care upon him for he careth for you." "Let the peace of God rule your hearts and minds," says Colossians 3:15. Fix your thoughts on God. Dispel the negative.

Casting every care on Him,
His keeping power through every hour is mine.
Though burdens press, my happy heart can sing;
Though fears dismay, I find His peace within.

Hebrews 4:9-11 says there is a positive level of peace and rest available to God's people. It says, "Let us" enter into that rest. We can live on a higher plane than those who don't know Christ. We can enter into a place of peace and rest where environment and circumstances don't throw us. Scientists are discovering new laws; we also need to discover God's laws for our well-being.

You Make Your Own Jail

Joseph was only 17 when a sensuous woman lied about him. He knew he had to live with his own conscience and his God. He spent 13 years, almost half of his young life, in jail, but he rose above those circumstances. He was in jail, but the jail wasn't in him!

In Danger

Two years ago we heard shouting and fighting on a dark street in Argentina. Then a shot rang out. My husband, Monnie, had just returned from Guayana. I had been alone for 5 weeks. I had sprained my ankle and it was very cold outside. He dashed into the street with his bedroom slippers and a sweater on.

There lay our neighbor, Guillermo, in a pool of blood. Monnie grabbed his 250-pound body, pulled it into our car, and sped to the hospital with Guillermo's wife, Lidia, at his side.

I went back inside the house and closed all five locks and turned the volume way up on the stereo, so if other assassins lurked in the dark they would think the house was full. I paced and prayed—peace came.

It was Guillermo's and Lidia's 22nd wedding anniversary. He was coming home to a special dinner with the family. He dropped a box of chocolates and a dozen carnations where he fell. Lidia had thought she had it made—a lovely brick home that had been completely remodeled, a nice garden.

Monnie returned home 2 hours later—it had been too late. Lidia was at my door each day wringing her hands.

A deep fear settled over the entire neighborhood. Leon, our Jewish neighbor, said, "I will move from here."

I asked him, "Where will you go where there is no fear? You take yourself along."

He did move—into an elegant marble-corridored apartment on the fourth floor. But 1 month later he had a near-fatal heart attack.

Alone

I knew I would have to be alone for months at a time while Monnie traveled teaching leadership seminars all over South America. How was I going to face the darkness? the night noises? How could I stand to be alone? to take my car and drive to the Bible school? to continue my teaching and training ministry? to continue to counsel others and uphold Lidia, alone?

I told the young Christians, "Yes, I've been afraid, but suddenly a blanket of peace has covered me. I am alone with peace."

Later I received a letter from a girlhood friend. She said, "Betty Jane, I was praying for you and the Lord directed me to Proverbs 3:23-26:

    —you will walk safely, your foot will not stumble

    —you will lie down and not be afraid

    —your sleep shall be sweet

—you will not be afraid of sudden fear

—the Lord will be your confidence and keep you."

She had prayed for me. God's peace came like a soft blanket.

Oh, the peace that Jesus gives
Never dies it always lives,
Like the music of a psalm
Like a glad eternal calm
Is the peace that Jesus gives,
Is the peace that Jesus gives.

How to Face It

Let's meet Jochebed, a woman in the Old Testament. Jochebed had a nagging suspicion that she was pregnant again: "Yes, just what I feared, it's over 3 months now." At night the thoughts troubled her. "I have Aaron and Miriam to care for—that is enough. And what if it is a boy? There is that terrible edict that all boys must be thrown in the river. How can I bear it?"

Jochebed's husband Amram was one of the Hebrew slaves. "Often Amram comes in at night with his back bleeding from the beatings the Egyptian guards give. This Amenotep Pharaoh is so worried about the Hykssos invading from the north. He's trying to decimate the Hebrew strength building those huge pyramids so there'll be no alliance."

She must have had 9 months of mental anguish, but when she saw her baby, she realized he was a special child. God had planned for him to be born so he could carry out a special assignment. "Oh, God, intervene so I can raise him. Don't let him be thrown in the river," she must have cried.

She hid him for 3 months. Every mother thinks her child is beautiful, but there was something special about this boy. The soldiers searched the homes of the Hebrews to kill the boy babies, but they did not find Jochebed's son. I wonder where she hid him? under their camel-hair bed? in a basket with the vegetables and onions in the kitchen?

As she nursed him, she talked to him, "You are given of God, you are special, you have a reason for being." She implanted peace and confidence in him. When he was 3 months old, she realized she couldn't hide him any longer. So, she gathered reeds from the river and, together with Miriam, wove a basket. She breathed a prayer with every reed. "Miriam, this is our baby; this is our project. God will use you to save your baby brother." She taught as they worked together.

Jochebed kissed her beautiful baby, prayed a prayer over him, and laid him in the basket. Then she and Miriam walked to the river. "Miriam, God will give you wisdom. He will show you what to do. I can't tell you what will happen, but God will guide you. God will watch over you and direct you."

Jochebed put her arm around Miriam's shoulder, left her in the reeds at the side of the river, and turned to go home.

How could she leave her two children in a place of danger? What would happen to them? She put her mind and heart at peace. She fixed her thoughts on God. She knew God was in control. She was a woman of grace.

How empty the little house seemed. She had a big lump in her throat. She cleaned away the rushes, started supper, and waited to see how God would work things out.

God was faithful. The princess came to bathe and heard a baby crying. He had waited until just the right moment to cry. Was this a coincidence? No, God orders even the minute details of our lives.

The princess saw the basket and realized that this was a Hebrew baby. "I will take him home; I found him." Just then Miriam stepped out of the reeds where she had been waiting. She offered the services of a nursemaid. I can imagine the emotion with which she ran to call her mother, "Mommy, Mommy, come quickly. The princess is calling for you. We can take our baby back home with us."

Jochebed came and saw her own baby in the arms of the princess. The princess said, "Go, nurse him, take care of him. I will pay you wages. I will call him Moses, or 'pulled out of the river.' "

The peace of God which passes all understanding flooded Jochebed's heart. She took her boy to her home, loved him, kissed him, talked to him, and trained him. "I must make every day count. I will have only about 5 years until I must take him back to the palace to grow up as the child of the princess."

Jochebed trained him. By the time he was weaned he knew who he was, why he was born, the history of the 400 years of captivity of the 12 sons of Jacob, why they were there in Egypt, and the purpose of God for His people. She imparted to him peace and faith in God. Jochebed had passed the peace of her life on to him in such measure that the Bible tells us Moses was the meekest man who ever lived. Peace from the cradle!

Moses wrote the Pentateuch, the first five Books of our Bible, and also Psalm 90, with its assurance: "Lord, thou hast been our dwelling place in all generations . . . even from everlasting to everlasting, thou art God . . . . So teach us to number our days that we may apply our hearts unto wisdom."

What if Miriam had whined, "I always have to help. I want to go play dolls. I get tired of standing in the reeds, my feet get wet."

Some mothers would say, "Poor dear, let her go."

Miriam learned obedience and responsibility at Jochebed's side. Many times we say, "It's too much bother to let them help. They make more work for me. I'd rather do it myself." "They get water all over the floor when they wash the dishes." "Run, watch TV!"

Who is responsible for a child's obedience? How much do you expect of your child?

Miriam was an important factor in Moses' life and salvation. Jochebed implanted peace and confidence in all three of her children. What a woman! Her oldest son became the first high priest for the nation; Miriam, the first prophetess and the song leader in times of discouragement; and Moses, the leader, law giver, and guide for the Hebrew nation. One woman drew on the peace of God and her life influenced the whole world through her three children.

In times of crisis our true character emerges. Only a woman with inner peace has clarity of thought.

Shh, Shh, Quiet

Psalm 131:2 says, "I have quieted my soul as a child that is weaned." Be still, my soul.

> *Peace, peace, wonderful peace,*
> *Coming down from the Father above,*
> *Sweep over my spirit forever I pray*
> *In fathomless billows of love.*

As we rest, we bring peace, rest, and quiet to those around us. James 3:18 says that the fruit of righteousness is sown in peace. If we are going to grow and bear fruit, we need peace within.

Thinking It Over Together

1. What did Jesus mean when He said, "Peace, be still?" What else could it mean?
2. What are the pressures that rob you of peace?

3. What can we do to feed a positive peaceful thought life?
4. Do we carry a storm center within us?
5. What kind of problems might a Christian face in today's society?
6. What is the resource God gives us for our problems?
7. What are the "ifs" you say each day?
8. How do you restore peace in a problem situation among your children?
9. Memorize John 14:27. Here is the true source of peace.

CHAPTER FIVE

Patience

Sarah, Time Heals All Wounds

GENESIS 12 to 22

I used to have a pastor who said, "Don't pray for patience. Pray for the working out of God's will in your life." Many times we know we need patience for a circumstance, a problem, or a decision.

But what is patience? It is firmness and constancy in the face of provocation. It is "the quality of enduring without complaint."

Actually *long-suffering* is the word used in the King James Version in the list of the fruit of the Spirit, but other versions use the word *patience*. In Colossians 1:11 the Word uses a trilogy, "Strengthened with all might . . . unto all patience and long-suffering with joyfulness." So God will give us strength to joyfully grow patience in our life garden.

Let's go to the Word of God. It seems that patience is related to suffering:

A. Suffering Creates Patience
 1. James 1:3, 4—"Knowing this, that the trying of your faith worketh patience. But let patience have her perfect work, that ye may be perfect and entire, wanting nothing."
 2. James 5:11—"Ye have heard of the patience of Job." This is a classic example. Job suffered much, yet in the end God was merciful.
 3. 1 Peter 2:20—"Ye take it patiently, this is acceptable with God."
 4. 1 Peter 5:10—"After that ye have suffered a

57

while, [God will] make you perfect, stablish, strengthen, settle you."

B. Growth Into Patience
1. 2 Peter 1:5-8—"Besides this, giving all diligence, add to your faith virtue; and to virtue, knowledge; and to knowledge, temperance; and to temperance, patience; and to patience, godliness. . . ."
2. Romans 5:3-5—"We glory in tribulations also: knowing that tribulation worketh patience; and patience experience; and experience, hope: and hope maketh not ashamed; because the love of God is shed abroad in our hearts by the Holy Ghost which is given unto us."

C. Example of the Farmer
1. James 5:7, 8—"Be patient therefore, brethren, unto the coming of the Lord. Behold the husbandman waiteth for the precious fruit of the earth, and hath long patience for it . . . . Be ye also patient; stablish your hearts: for the coming of the Lord draweth nigh."
2. The harvest doesn't ripen in 2 weeks or in a month. Some trees take 3 years before they produce fruit; others, like the papaya, bear fruit in a few months. You must know which fruit you are planting. Patience takes longer than some of the other fruit. Be quiet, be still, possess your souls. Patience will have its perfection.

D. Example of a Race
1. Hebrews 12:1, 2—"Run with patience the race that is set before us, looking unto Jesus the author and finisher of our faith; who for the joy that was set before him endured the cross, despising the shame, and is set down at the right hand of the throne of God."

This is a paradox. How can we run a race with patience? If we're going to run, we have to get on our mark, get set, go! To run with patience is to run with a quiet heart. With our eyes straight ahead and our face set like a flint, our goal is a life of usefulness for Christ.

2. Hebrews 10:36—"Ye have need of patience, that after ye have done the will of God, ye might receive the promise." After we have obeyed and waited, then in God's time comes the prize.

E. Necessary Quality for Ministers

1. 2 Corinthians 6:4—"Approving ourselves as the ministers of God, in much patience, in afflictions, in necessities, in distresses . . . ."

2. 2 Corinthians 4:17, 18—"For our light affliction, which is but for a moment, worketh for us a far more exceeding and eternal weight of glory; while we look not at the things which are seen, but at the things which are not seen: for the things which are seen are temporal; but the things which are not seen are eternal." It's worth being patient to gain the eternal reward.

3. Revelation 2:2, 3—"I know thy works, and thy labor and thy patience . . . and for my name's sake [thou] hast labored, and has not fainted."

4. 1 Timothy 6:11—"Follow after righteousness, godliness, faith, love, patience, meekness."

Thus, we see that none of the fruit grows independently. All are interrelated and intertwined. When there is godliness, faith, and love in the life, then patience and meekness also grow.

There is a Spanish idiom that is often used: "Pa-

ciencia y buen humor." "Patience and good humor."
If we can keep our good humor, patience will grow.
If we can be quiet and wait a little, good humor will
surface.

Sit Down

A mother was trying to tame her unruly son.
"Johnny, sit down there in the corner with your face
turned until you can be quiet." He jumped up, for-
getting. "Johnny, I said sit down." He plopped down
pouting, "Well, I'm still standing up inside."

In Watchman Nee's book *Sit, Walk, Stand* he says:
"It is impossible for us to learn to walk in the spirit
until we learn to 'sit down' with Jesus as in Ephesians
2:6." To sit down, to relax, to quiet ourselves is basic
for learning patience in our lives.

Slow to Lose Patience

Recently when our daughter Mona Re' was expecting her first baby, she was alone in her apartment.
(Her husband Mike is a busy pastor.) We were 10,000
miles away in Argentina. Her sister Rachel came for
her due date, but the baby didn't cooperate. Rachel
finally had to return home to her minister husband in
Michigan.

Fifteen days, twenty days, forty days—you can imagine how our patience was being tested! Every time
we'd return home from a week away in a Sunday
school convention or a youth retreat, we'd wonder if
the baby had come.

Finally, Mike called from Minnesota. Kristin Rachel
had arrived 50 days late.

Mona wrote: "The Lord taught me to quiet myself,
to wait, and to be a better person. I looked at my
baby, her perfection, and my mind went back to those

days in the country mountains of Bolivia where we would all go to teach together.

"I remembered that terrible cold. I would boil water on the kerosene stove for the water bottle for my feet. My little bunk in the trailer was hard and cold. Our hands were so chapped and cracked. Remember the Vaseline we put around our ears and nose to keep them moistened in that cold? I thought of the heaping mountains of rice we ate as we shared the hot peppery supper with the Indian students. How I went into class early in the morning to teach the men to read and write. But I have no regrets, for through the hardness of sharing in your ministry in the country—I am learning patience. I look again at my baby, and I have no regrets."

Impatience

To have patience is to quietly await the fulfillment of God's plan for our lives. This is difficult for us. Too many of us say, "When do I want it? I wanted it yesterday!"

Patience is a lesson we will keep on learning until we see our Master face to face and He says, "Well done, receive your prize for the race you have run."

Now I want to share with some of you lovely girls who are still waiting for God to reveal the companion of His choice. Marriage is like finding the other half of the orange, or like knowing for sure we are the missing rib of that certain someone. I feel it is important to pray from the time we know the Lord that He will also guard the companion He has for us. In marriage we must be very certain of God's guidance, for it is for life.

Haste Makes Waste

Living is an art, not an exact science, so it is necessary to wait and be patient. It is much better to live a happy, contented life alone and serve God with freedom, than to choose wrong and be married to someone who hampers our serving God.

There are many completely fulfilled women who choose to serve God as single women. They have a ministry and an important place in God's plan. So we mustn't equate happiness with finding a marriage partner. Contentment and patience must grow, as Paul says, "in whatsoever state I find myself"!

God Speaks to Us

I have some Scripture passages marked in my Bible through which God spoke to me when I was going through problems and needed patience to see the other side. I have dates written in the margins. I can see how God made a map for me through the Word—May 1943, January 1955, August 1969, June 1977. . . .

In Psalm 40:1-4 the Psalmist says, "I waited patiently for the Lord; he inclined unto me and heard my cry." God helped him, put his feet on a rock, and put a new song in his heart. He is our God; we will praise Him!

Psalm 27:13, 14 says: "I had fainted unless I had believed to see the goodness of the Lord in the land of the living. Wait on the Lord: be of good courage, and he shall strengthen thine heart: Wait . . . ." Here this thought of waiting is underscored. This is how patience is perfected in us.

David actually talks to his soul in Psalm 62:5-8. This helps me, for I find at times I have to quiet my soul, "My soul, wait thou only upon God; . . . trust in him . . . pour out your heart before him; God is a refuge for us."

* * * * *

A woman feels a deep need for security; to have roots that go down deep. She longs to have friends, family, and a home, and live without fear, confident that all is well in her surroundings.

Sarai felt very secure in Ur. Abram was successful. In today's terms, they were of the wealthy class, with no financial problems, a lovely home, and good standing in the community. They had security.

Then one evening Abram came home and said, "Sarai, I had a visitor today, a heavenly visitor. He said we should leave here, move out, and look for a new country whose builder and maker is God."

Sarai could well have asked, "And what did he look like? What did he say and where are we going? How long will it take?"

"Patience, Sarai, I don't know the answers to your questions. I only know God has called me and I must obey. Will you come along with me?"

The full story of Sarai walking with Abram covers 12 chapters in Genesis. Then in verses 8-11 of Hebrews 11 (which is known as "The Faith Chapter"), we have a concise flashback of the entire drama.

"Will I go? Can I leave my home? What about my garden? my pets? my cousins? my friends? Where are we going? He doesn't even know. How far? How long will it take?" These are questions women ask today, just as Sarai must have asked them of Abram.

"I don't know, Abram. I have lived here since I was a girl. You brought me to this house as a bride. I grew up here and now you say we're going somewhere —you don't even know where—you have heard a voice and you must follow. That's rather ethereal isn't it? No map, no road, no real indications. We'll be following a voice. How will we know when we arrive?"

"All right, Abram, I have pledged my love to you,

that where you go I will go; that I will love, honor, cherish, and obey; so I will go."

I can imagine that Sarai had a last big dinner to inform her neighbors, family, and friends. She used her lovely things for the last time. Then she started to pack—just the necessary items to make a new home; no excess baggage. She folded her flowing silk robes. They sold and gave away their furniture.

She may have dug up some of the flowers that had bloomed in her garden and shared them with special friends. She probably had a lump in her throat as she made all the decisions for leaving.

They took the herds, camels, cattle, and sheep along. Abram had a special tent made. Sarai learned to ride a camel. They left everything that had been her security.

By faith, Abram was "called" to go out. He "obeyed"—not knowing where he was going. He "sojourned," or lived, in a strange land, "dwelt" in tents, "looked for" a city, "was persuaded," "believed," and "waited."

This same faith helped to make Sarai a great woman of patience. Abram had heard the voice, but Sarai believed Abram.

Sarai was a beautiful woman. Several times other men and kings of the countries in which they were traveling recognized her beauty. She was rather obstinate and headstrong, but it seems Sarai and Abram talked things over. That always helps.

No Map

They started up the Euphrates River. If they had crossed the desert it would have been about 700 miles, but Abram followed the river so they would have water and food for the herds—so it took a long time. Abram's father, Terah, died in Haran and then they moved on to fulfill God's will. Abram was 75 and Sarai was 65, so neither was young.

One day God appeared to Abram again and told him that he and Sarai would have descendants as numerous as the sands of the sea and as the stars, and all the nations of the world would be blessed through their posterity. He changed their names to Abraham and Sarah when Abraham was 99 years old (Genesis 17:5, 15).

Sarah, whose new name meant "Princess," was eavesdropping at the door of the tent. She laughed when she heard Abraham's visitors promise him a son. But the Lord said to Abraham, "Wherefore did Sarah laugh? . . . Is anything too hard for the Lord?" (Genesis 18:13, 14).

Sarah must have thought to herself, "How can that be true? I've traveled all these miles, living in that goat-hair tent, having no one but servants to talk with. I've been very much alone—not even a child to teach. I have passed the time of menopause. My body is no longer young; my tissues are shriveling. Me have a baby! How can that be?"

But Sarah caught the faith to believe and "bare Abraham a son in his old age, at the set time of which God had spoken" (21:2). She named him Isaac, which means "Laughter," for she said, "Many will laugh and be joyous with me for I have borne a son!"

Possibly we wouldn't think of Sarah as a patient woman, but I like the thought that she *learned* patience. She heard the promise. She obeyed Abraham. She kept her faith strong. And finally she saw the fruition of all those years of traveling and believing.

When they started their journey her name was Sarai which meant "Contentious." But this proud, stubborn, haughty, beautiful woman let the fruit of patience grow until God could even change her name to "Princess." She was transformed in the desert.

Moving Sale—Sacrifice

Today's families are on the move. Statistics say that one family in five will move this year. Deep within her heart, a woman would rather keep her roots down, make friends, and feel secure.

Recently a friend wrote me: "Like a good army wife, I'm actually looking forward to this move and to making new friends and a new home." She had worked hard and made a lovely home. Now her military husband had a new assignment. She had caught the right spirit—a spirit of teaming up with her husband to make their life together the best possible.

Women have to move for various reasons. Classified ads in almost every newspaper include the words, "Moving sale, sacrifice."

It's really hard to start to dig in for moving. When our ministry changed, we sorted through 25 years of life in South America to pack and move our home and office to Miami. I found the box that contained our love letters from before our marriage, written 32 years ago; the box with the old family photographs; the ribbon from my wedding bouquet. I found my wedding gown with the little white lace gloves; the box with Rachel's Barbie dolls; Mona's paints from 16 years of school and painting lessons; Rocky's fossils, rocks, and articles; and special greeting cards and poetry.

One box had the little red shoes Mona had learned to walk in, her first baby spoon, and a hand-crocheted blanket. I found letters from my mother inspiring faith and telling of her prayers for us during those early years of our missionary service. There were records, music books, and special studies I had taught.

Where do you start? What do you keep? What do

you sell? What do you give away? I know many of you have been through this too.

In fact, as we returned to the states after our decisions were made, I found our son's house in the same situation. They were following the Voice to go, to leave, to obey, to follow. They were leaving everything and going to Argentina as missionaries. They were making the same decisions.

Just like Sarah—following God without a map. When we are able to see the map and the calendar, it seems we can believe and have patience. God made Hebrews 10:36 real to me when I was a young girl: "You have need of patience, after having done the will of God, to receive the promise thereof." First, we obey, then we have patience—then comes the fulfillment and the prize.

The race is not always to the swift, nor the battle to the strong. The race is won by patience—by sticking with it and learning to walk with God, step by step, without a map.

> *If I walk in the pathway of duty,*
> *If I work till the close of the day,*
> *I shall see the great King in His beauty*
> *When I've gone the last mile of the way.*

* * * * *

Let's Check up on Ourselves

1. What are the signs of impatience in the line at the supermarket?
2. Why would an impatient woman be more accident prone?
3. Why does the Word say that tribulation works patience?
4. How might a farmer show impatience?
5. How is the patience of Job shown in the Bible?

6. What was the reward for Job's patience?
7. What were some of the problems and trials that created patience in Sarah's life?
8. When was the last time you were impatient?
9. What is your attitude toward a change of plans?
10. Practice makes perfect. How can we develop the Spirit's fruit of patience in our life garden?
11. Have you marked some of the Scripture passages from this chapter in your Bible? They will help you.

CHAPTER SIX

Gentleness

Hannah, Misjudged but Unruffled

1 SAMUEL 1 and 2

A nurse was washing a new mother's face in the hospital shortly after her delivery. "Do you have a family?" the lady asked.

"Oh, yes, I have two little boys," replied the nurse.

"I thought so from the way you're scouring my face," the new mother complained.

What about your manner? Are you gentle? Do you have a soft touch? Are you rough? Is your voice gruff? Are you sharp in your demeanor? They say a barking dog won't bite and a gruff person has a tender heart. But we're not drawn to either one. Jesus said, "Learn of me, for I am meek and lowly." He is gentle and has a tender Spirit. He wants us to be like Him.

Full of Grace

"The fruit of the Spirit is . . . gentleness." Gentleness is love refined. It is actually shown in our treatment of children, older people, those less fortunate, and animals. To be kind in the little things is an almost forgotten form of behavior. It is to say, "Thank you for the good supper," and, "Excuse me, please," when we leave the table. It is to be respectful, thoughtful, gracious, and considerate. The gentle woman is a woman of grace and courtesy.

Ephesians 4:32 teaches us how to be gentle: "Be ye kind one to another, tender-hearted, forgiving one another, even as God for Christ's sake hath forgiven you." We learned to quote this early in our family.

Actually, the bustling, fast-moving life we live today tends to make even some Christians annoyed. We're always in a hurry. We're impatient with people, discourteous, and sharp. To have a gentle nature is not easy today, but let us learn to be gentle women by God's grace. We are studying the fruit of the Spirit. The Spirit wants us to have gentleness growing in our life garden.

I remember my father's hands. He had only half a left hand after a grain elevator accident. But they were tender hands. When I fell while ice skating and cracked my head open, he brought an ice pack and gently placed it on the injury. He brought me tea. He changed the cotton. He knew how to make a soft bandage.

When I was getting dressed before my piano recital, he took time to gently tie the big bow on my silk sash. He made the folds lie just right. When he knew of criticism and misunderstanding leveled against me, he always had a gentle, kind, wise word, "Time heals all wounds."

First Thessalonians 2:7 says, "We were gentle among you, even as a nurse cherisheth her children." Ah, the gentle touch of a cool hand on a fevered brow; the nights spent by the side of a sick child—the fruit that is gentleness of spirit refreshes others.

Insecurity

There is a lot of talk today of sibling rivalry. I believe this goes back to the parent's attitude. We can prepare a child to receive the new baby. Don't make room for jealousy. Involve your child in the preparations. Let him know you are waiting for "our" baby.

Remember the story of Miriam as she helped prepare the basket for Moses? This made her responsible to protect him. It gave her a gentle nature. A child who pinches or bites a new baby shows insecurity. We can help him, through gentleness in our own nature.

In Bill Sands' book *My Shadow Ran Fast,* he tells how his mother whipped him with a long thorny cactus branch. Her sadism created such a rebellion in his heart that although his father was the wealthy city judge, he decided to become a criminal. He recounts the long road to delinquency which started from the lack of gentleness at home.

I believe affection should be openly expressed in a home. This is God's plan. Children will grow up accepting and being able to give affection if there is an open wholesome attitude of affection at home. At times our own natural stubborn nature dictates that we should be sour, rough, rude, and hard-boiled, but the seed of gentleness is sown in kindness.

The Word Teaches Us

A. David Had a Gentle Nature
   1. 2 Samuel 18:5—"Deal gently with . . . Absalom."
   2. 2 Samuel 22:36—"Thy gentleness has made me great." David was a man after God's own heart, although a warrior.
B. The Servant of the Lord Must Be Gentle
   1. Isaiah 40:10, 11—"He will come with strong hand . . . and shall gently lead those that are with young."
   2. Isaiah 42:1-3—"A bruised reed shall he not break."
   3. 2 Timothy 2:24—"The servant of the Lord must not strive; but be gentle unto all men, apt to teach, patient."

71

4. Titus 3:2—"Speak evil of no man, . . . gentle, showing all meekness unto all men."

C. Our Adornment as a Woman
   1. 1 Peter 3:4—"The ornament of a meek and quiet spirit."
   2. Colossians 3:12, 13—"Put on . . . kindness . . . meekness."

D. Gentleness Is Wisdom
   1. James 3:17—"The wisdom that is from above is first pure, then peaceable, gentle, and easy to be entreated, full of mercy, and good fruits."
   2. Colossians 4:9—Walk in wisdom; lead a gentle life.

The following is a list of things that characterize gentleness, and those that do not:

Not	*But Rather*
outward adornment	a meek, quiet spirit
rough	gentle
striving, brawler	easy to be entreated
haughty	lowly, meek
speaking evil	words of wisdom
works of righteousness	mercy
bitterness, envying, strife	peaceableness, gentleness
confusion	peace
earthly, devilish	pure, heavenly
partiality, hypocrisy	good fruits
corruptible	eternal
sensual	full of good works

The Shepherd's Nature

In Isaiah we find two pictures of Jesus. First, we see Him as the Shepherd. He picks up the wounded one; He is gentle, He guides, He cares, and He tenderly leads. The second picture we see of Christ is that of a servant. He doesn't break a bruised reed or quench smoking flax.

Sometimes we find our young people teeter-tottering between doing God's will and being stubborn, recalcitrant, going their own way, and following the crowd. By our attitude we can give them a push in either direction. If we are caustic, surly, bitter, and critical of God's people, their decision may be toward the world.

When their reed is already bruised, may we find it in us to be gentle and tender, to come alongside, tie up the young plants, and be there for them to lean on. Instead of crushing the life out of the bruised ones, let us encourage, lift, and nurse them toward God.

Use Your Golden Scissors to Trim

All through the Word we see where the instruments God fashions are of gold (as in the tabernacle). Gold is a type of divinity, a touch of God's character. When the flax of the wick was smoking, the priest used his golden scissors and lifted the wick with golden tongs and tenderly cut away the carbon, shaping it to a perfect form, rather than quenching the flickering, smoking flame.

God doesn't mean for us to lose our personality or our individualism. He made us and He wants to use us. He carefully trims away the burnt parts. Thus He teaches us to deal tenderly with others—to be women of grace. Let us be careful how we correct others.

I Watched Your Gentle Nature

"When I first came to Bible college, I kept watching the people around me. I found some were rough; they huffed and puffed. Others had straw natures, blowing in the wind. Then I watched Rocky. His quiet dignity and gentleness made me know that if he could do it, I could too. I thank God for his example."

So wrote a young man who watched our son and later married our daughter. No one lives to himself. No one dies to himself. We have a great sphere of influence. When we receive letters that say, "I watched your life, I needed the gentleness, the quiet way you spoke. It was balm to my wounded spirit," we are encouraged to continue to be gentle.

Gentle Shepherd, come and help us,
For we need Thy tender care.

Sweetness Under Provocation

"Why are you coming drunk to the church, Hannah? Learn to handle your liquor."

"Oh, no, I haven't been drinking. My soul is full of anguish. I've been talking to God about my problem."

Eli the priest had cruelly misjudged Hannah. But she was accustomed to taunts, ridicule, and being misjudged. She lived with it every day. She knew her husband, Elkanah, loved her, but they had no children. So she was asking God for a son. Her barrenness was the reason Elkanah's second wife, Peninnah, scorned her so. She had several children and Hannah had none. Their house was full of rivalry and taunts.

And now even God's man in His temple had misjudged her. "Oh, God, give me a son for Thy sake. I will give him back to You. I will dedicate him to You."

So Eli answered, "What you have asked, you will receive. Go in faith."

Joy bubbled in Hannah's gentle heart. She washed her face and ate with great appetite. Food hadn't tasted good for so long. The heaviness of her heart lifted. The pilgrims returned home and before long Hannah knew God had answered her prayer. She was expecting a child.

We know the story of Hannah's son, Samuel, and how God called him in the night. Samuel was the promised child and his name means "Asked of God."

Hannah trained him well at home. She loved him, counseled him, instructed him, and guided him until the day she weaned him. She remembered her promise to give him back to God. He was a young child when they left him in the temple to serve Eli and God.

I can imagine Hannah as she returned home. The house was quiet. There was no longer the patter of little feet. It seemed so empty. But Hannah sang, "My heart rejoices in the Lord." She kept gentleness in her spirit, knowing that God was over all. Each year she made a new little coat and took it to Samuel. God honored her gentle spirit and gave her three more sons and two daughters.

Hannah realized the importance of those early years of training Samuel. She must have passed her gentle nature on to him. If she had filled him full of bitterness against Peninnah, he couldn't have ministered before the Lord. Hannah taught him correctly.

So Much to Learn

Child psychologists tell us a child learns half of all he'll ever know by the end of his 3rd year. It seems incredible, but think about it. What does a baby know at birth? How to cry, suck, and grab.

A baby learns very early how to get approval, warmth, love, and contentment. He also learns fear or hatred. Thank God for the homes that *don't* teach it! He can detect fear in a person's voice. We teach by the way we speak to him.

A baby learns to eat with a spoon and to know the

75

tastes of different foods. What he doesn't like he spits out! He learns to balance himself, to stand, to walk, to fall, to get back up, to focus his eyes, to say syllables and words, and to sing, pray, and repeat.

It was such fun to have our granddaughter Kristi with us for a few days when she was 9 months old. Whenever she was tired and cross I would say, "Let's la-la-la, Kristi." She would listen, quiet herself, and then sing, "La-la." We can teach our children to have a joyful heart; to sing their cares away.

Proverbs 22:6 tells us to train up a child in the way he should go and when he is old he won't depart from it. He will continue to walk in the correct path if he's trained from an early age.

Hannah followed an important recipe for child rearing in her treatment of Samuel. Deuteronomy 6:5-9 tells us we first must love God with all our heart, soul, and might; then we must teach these precepts to our children.

It says we should talk about God's Word in our house—while walking and lying down, morning and night. We are to write it on the walls of our homes and on the memories of our children. It is important that we talk about the Lord to our children, read the Word together, and commit the day into God's hands. We should pray at the table over the food, and pray and commit ourselves to His protection at all times.

It is important to memorize the Word together. One very effective way is to play Bible games. We used to travel many miles visiting churches. We played a game with our three children in the back seat. We said, "I'm thinking of . . . ," and they had to identify the Bible character, based on the answers we gave to the questions they asked about him.

There are many steps in raising a child to be a complete person. First we are to tell him, then teach him (which means being an example), and then work with him, correct him, and discipline him.

In our study of the fruit of "joy," we mentioned the roulette wheel of genetic inheritance. There is the fusion of 46 chromosomes, 23 from each parent. From this new cell which creates a person, there are 15 million possible combinations of characteristics. We inherit our temperament; we develop our character; and we refine our personality, which is the part of us that others see and know.

It is important to remember that the grace of God can change any temperament, and walking in the Spirit can refine any character or personality. We can grow the fruit of gentleness as we walk in the Spirit.

Jesus loved John. It seems he had a gentle nature, although he was one of the "sons of thunder." While on the cross, Jesus remembered Mary, His mother, and asked John to take her and care for her as his own mother.

TLC

God cares about us. Matthew 6:25-34 tells us He watches the sparrows and knows when they fall. He watches over the lilies and knows when they bloom. He also watches over us. Gently He cares for us. He loves us—we are His children. Because God loves us, we can manifest "tender loving care" to others.

Gentleness in Marriage

Do you like to see an older couple holding hands? We do too. Have you ever seen a couple sitting at a table in a restaurant, completely oblivious of each other? One may be looking out the window, the other reading the paper or looking around. They seem to be trying to avoid each other even though they are together.

How does a woman create and keep gentleness alive in her marriage? Add your own suggestions to this partial list:

Keep a gentle tongue

Adapt your way of being to his desires

Fix the foods he likes

Have the table set and ready when he arrives

In honor, preferring one another

Keep your body clean, not just perfumed

Be interested in the things he enjoys

Gentleness to the Less Fortunate

What do you do if you see a blind person waiting with his white cane for the light to change? Do you rush right on by? Or do you take a minute to gently offer assistance? He may not want or need it, but your gentle attention will brighten his day.

How do you react to a mentally deficient person who wants to chat with you? Do you extend your hand, shake hands, and treat him with dignity? How do you treat those in your neighborhood who are less fortunate than you? They too have souls. They can be won to Christ through gentleness and kindness.

To All Men

I remember an evangelist friend. He spoke to crowds of 10,000 people in a stadium. But he was just as attentive to a little Indian widow who was speaking with him as he was when he talked with the President of the Republic. His whole attention was given to each person.

My prayer for you is that the gentle nature of Christ will be yours as you live and walk in the Spirit.

Taking Inventory of Our Garden

1. How do you react to the person who is mentally deficient?

2. If the car ahead of you is slow to move when the light changes, what do you do?

3. When you see some of the young people from your church engaging in questionable practices, what is your reaction? Have you ever thought of helping to open a recreation center or game room?

4. If there is a problem in your church, how can you guard your children so the root of bitterness will not grow in their lives?

5. Is there anything in your life that calls for as great a sacrifice as Hannah made?

6. What contemporary problems do women face that are similar to the problems in Hannah's home?

CHAPTER SEVEN

Goodness

Phoebe, We Can Count on You

ROMANS 16

"Johnny, be good."

"Jane, be good." "Be good now."

"The fruit of the Spirit is . . . goodness." What does it mean? Be good? One little boy went to school and when they were making up the class roll they asked his name. He replied, "Johnny Don't." He had trouble being "good."

"Goodness" comes from the word *good*. It means genuine, wholesome, pure, truthful, upright, chaste, prudent, correct, and honorable. Do you know anyone that is full of goodness?

Psalm 37:23 is so beautiful: "The steps of a good man are ordered by the Lord; and he delighteth in his way." Before we know Christ there is no goodness in us, but when we walk in the Spirit, one step at a time, goodness grows. Walking in the Spirit frees us of our natural weaknesses.

We have just studied gentleness. How would you say that gentleness and goodness can be compared? How are they different? It would seem that gentleness is what our inward character is. We can have a gentle nature. Goodness is the outward manifestation of that inward character in our relationships with others.

Transformed

Juana was a Japanese woman who was saved in the Evangelistic Center in La Paz, Bolivia. She owned a restaurant down the mountainside. She was partially paralyzed. One leg, one arm, and one hand were crippled from a fall off the gangplank of a boat in Japan when she was 3 years old. Juana testified that before she knew the Lord, she had been so mean. The children would laugh at her and call her names because she dragged one foot. But after accepting Jesus that meanness and bad nature was so transformed that the children would run to her.

She was a talented seamstress and she made shirts for the pastors. As the fruit of goodness grew in her life, she became an excellent teacher of the beginner class. Meanness was transformed into goodness.

Let's turn to Titus 2:1-14 for our study of goodness. I will quote it from J. B. Phillips' translation:

"Now you must tell them the sort of character which should spring from sound teaching. The old men should be temperate, serious, wise—spiritually healthy through their faith and love and patience. Similarly the old women should be reverent in their behavior, should not make unfounded complaints and should not be overfond of wine. They should be examples of the good life, so that the younger women may learn to love their husbands and their children, to be sensible and chaste, homelovers, kind hearted and willing to adapt themselves to their husbands—a good advertisement for the Christian faith.

"The young men too, you should urge to take life seriously, letting your own life stand as a pattern of good living. In all your teaching show the strictest regard for truth, and show that you appreciate the seriousness of the matters you are dealing with. Your speech should be unaffected and logical, so that your opponent may feel ashamed at finding nothing in which to pick holes.

"Slaves should be told that it is their duty as Christians to obey their masters and to give them satisfactory service in every way. They are not to 'answer back' or to be light-fingered, but they are to show themselves utterly trustworthy, a living testimonial to the teaching of God their Saviour.

"For the grace of God, which can save every man, has now become known, and it teaches us to have no more to do with godlessness or the desires of this world but to live, here and now, responsible, honorable and God-fearing lives. And while we live this life we hope and wait for the glorious *dénouement* of God himself and of Jesus Christ our Saviour. For he gave himself for us all, that he might rescue us from all our evil ways and make for himself a people of his own, clean and pure, with our hearts set upon living a life that is good."

This gives us a big responsibility. As women we need to be teachers of the good. We must realize we are being watched. As the saying goes: "What you do speaks so loudly I can't hear what you say." Our lives are the best advertisement for the gospel.

You Are Transparent

A girl said to me after I'd spoken about the importance of a mother's teaching in the home, "If only my mother could have heard this teaching. If only she had lived in the home what she testified in the women's meetings—that's why I'm lost today, bitter and rebellious." Mothers, we are transparent.

There is a spiritual attractiveness in just plain goodness. Live prudently. Be careful how you live, dress, and speak. Be careful how you talk about your husband. It's easy to say, "Oh, that husband of mine never listens to me. He's just impossible." But someone may pick up that remark and blow it all out of proportion. His goodness and our own can be blemished by careless remarks.

Don't talk unkindly about each other. Don't talk to your in-laws about the little faults you find. Don't tell your children, "You know your father is so careless. . . ." *Shhh.*

Goodness shows in many ways. It is reflected in the way you keep your home and your body neat and clean. Don't wear sweaty, torn T-shirts and overalls around. Ask the Holy Spirit to help you show goodness to your children.

One facet of goodness is good judgment. Be wise with the intimate things between you and your husband. This is part of being chaste.

Keep a comfortable, attractive home. We are teachers of the good. Teach your children to do the right things. Sometimes we talk so much *about* our child; we need to talk *to* him in training and teaching him about goodness.

Don't "Answer Back"

Do you know someone who is always mumbling under her breath? never in accord with decisions that are made? Sometimes you hear women who are helping for a special banquet or fellowship meeting at the church groaning among themselves in the kitchen. Like Martha. We had a girl who lived with us for many years. I could hear her grumbling to the pots and pans! We are to do with all our willingness and might whatever our hands find to do. We are to adorn the gospel!

Dependable!

I want to show you another woman of grace. She was a single woman who was a deaconess in the church of Cenchrea, the important seaport of Corinth.

According to *Halley's Bible Handbook* and other

sources, Phoebe was the bearer of Paul's letter to the Romans. To paraphrase the introduction of Phoebe in Romans 16:1-3, we might read:

I'm sending this letter to you Italians by the hand of Phoebe. She is our sister and a hard worker in the church. She is always helping someone and is known for her good works. Anyone who knocks on her door, sailor or pilgrim, she takes in and helps them. She has helped me many times. She is a worthy, intelligent business woman.

Isn't this a warm picture that Paul gives us? In this special letter, he tells the Italian Jews to be transformed by the renewing of their minds; not to be conformed to the world, but to be ready to present their bodies as a living sacrifice. Then he closes the letter with the introduction of Phoebe and with warm personal greetings to a whole list of friends. It seems that nearly half the people he remembers by name in a special way in this last chapter are women. He placed this letter in Phoebe's hands because he knew she was dependable. She fulfilled the picture we have studied in Titus 2. The fruit of goodness was in her life. He could trust her.

Let's look at the other women he mentions here.

Phoebe's Friends

He sends greetings to Priscilla and Aquila. They were special helpers in the work and had even risked their lives for Paul. Verse 6 speaks of Mary who had worked very hard and was given to hospitality and good works.

In verse 12 come the twins, Tryphena and Tryphosa, who worked alongside Persis. Then he sends special greetings to Rufus, who was "chosen in the

Lord.'' It would seem that Rufus was black, as his father, Simon the Cyrene, was the one who helped Jesus carry the cross (Mark 15:21).

I can imagine the scene as Simon returned late the evening of the Crucifixion and said: ''My dear wife, you'll pardon me for being so late, but I was involved in the strangest event this afternoon. They pushed the cross of a condemned man onto my shoulders. I walked along by His side. He didn't groan, He didn't wince. He walked with dignity as if He knew where He was going and why. I watched while they pounded nails into His hands and feet, and then they pierced His side. It was uncanny, the darkness that came down. I'll never be the same again. I believe that this was the Son of God.''

Rufus could have been listening. I remember when as a child we would hear the fire engine go by, we'd all jump on our bikes to go see what was happening. I think Rufus did this. He slipped out the door and up the hill. He had to see for himself. He may have arrived in time to hear Jesus cry, ''Father, forgive them for they know not what they do.'' Maybe he saw the Roman soldiers throw dice for His woven, seamless robe.

Paul says that Rufus was chosen in the Lord, and his mother became as a mother to Paul. She mended his tunic, fixed him special meals, prayed for him, and welcomed him. Paul says, ''Your mother, Rufus, and mine.'' These were the women around Phoebe— all of them helping—women filled with goodness. This is why the gospel spread. There were women who ministered of their means and with their hands and heart.

And You?

There is a place for every woman. There is a ministry in the fruit of goodness.

I was teaching at North Central Bible College during a furlough when my father called to say my mother was to have exploratory surgery.

I said, "Daddy, I'll be there. If I were in Bolivia I couldn't come home. But tomorrow I'll be in Rapid City on the first plane of the morning."

After the surgery the doctors gave her just a short time to live.

When I saw my mother in that hospital bed, for the first time I noticed her hands. She had fine, well-shaped, attractive hands. She had used them in Shakespearian dramatization, but I had always seen them beating a cake, chopping cabbage for slaw, or kneading bread. They were lovely, helping hands—hands of service.

She said, "I have no ministry."

"Ah, Mother, you have no pulpit, you have no classroom, but you have an extended ministry."

I remembered that when a young preacher's mobile home burned, Mother was the first to pile blankets, pillows, sheets, canned foods, milk, and meat into the car and go 35 miles to help.

After the Sunday service she would watch to see who needed an invitation. Since we lived in an air-base town, the most attractive fellows would be invited first by other families. Those who were left were invited by Mother. Our home was always open.

I remembered the missionaries with their big rusty trunks scratching the newly varnished floor of my bedroom while I slept on the couch in the living room. There was room for everyone.

"Mother, your gift is in 1 Corinthians 12:28. In the list right along with tongues, miracles, pastors, and preachers, there is the ministry gift *helps*. You have always been a helping hand extended with anointed ministry. All your children are finding ways of ministering because you shared and showed the way."

Six months later when we buried Mother, the women wept as they cleaned the church and fixed the coleslaw, "Betty Jane, this is the last time we can minister to her. Your mother led the way, she ministered to so many."

She wasn't on any committees, her name wasn't in the bulletin, she wasn't an officer, and she didn't have an important position. I often found her on her knees in a little warm corner. She had decided to pour her life out as an extended hand. She was a woman of grace, full of goodness and used of God.

> *Oh, to be His hand extended*
> *Reaching out to the oppressed,*
> *Let me touch Him, let me touch Jesus*
> *So that others will know and be blessed.*

Obey the Nudge

I think here is the place for that special "nudge" of the Spirit. I knew a woman whose home was like an accordion. Sometimes there were just their four children in the two bedrooms, but other times there were evangelists in each bedroom, Bible school students sleeping on the couch, visiting deacons in a room out back, and the children in sleeping bags.

You could always count on her serving a cup of tea with a happy heart. Just as Phoebe, she succoured many. That's an old English word but it means she was a helper; a friend who aided many.

I remember one afternoon I was especially impressed that I should bake a cake and go visit a missionary friend in Argentina. My husband was teaching in Colombia, so I was alone. I was convalescing from a serious surgery and didn't feel well. But this impression kept coming. So I said, "Tomorrow I will go."

"No, *today*," the Spirit urged.

So I baked a cake—it fell. It looked like a camel

between humps. Again I said, "Tomorrow." I remembered my mother used to say you can correct a poor cake with a good frosting, so I tried that. The frosting ran all over because of the humidity, so again I said, "Tomorrow."

The Spirit kept insisting, so when my daughter came home from school, I said, "What about going to visit our friend Haydee?"

"Great, Mommy. Let's go."

It meant traveling 10 miles in a rickety bus, when I didn't feel well. So I took my sloppy crooked cake, picked up a new book I had, got some flowers from the yard, and we went to the bus.

When I climbed the stairs to where my friend lay in bed trying to save a pregnancy, she looked at me and said, "Jane, who told you it was my birthday?"

How could I have known? Her parents were missionaries in Africa, her sister was in Canada, and the Spirit had said, "Go and minister to My servant." Obey the nudging of the Spirit, He's always on time!

As goodness develops in the garden of our life we are kinder, more giving, and more understanding.

Simple Concerning Evil

At the end of his letter, in Romans 16:19, Paul says we should be wise to that which is good and simple concerning evil. This is a very important and timely word for women. We need to be wise to discern how to grow good fruit. What can help us?

Music has a powerful influence in our world today. We should have good music in our homes. We can teach our children while they are very young to sing happy songs, choruses, carols, and hymns. There are many wonderful records and cassettes available to bring an atmosphere of peace and goodness into our homes. We can offset the empty, often evil music they hear by filling our homes with good music.

"You Are What You Read"

As a young girl I read my father's copy of *In His Steps,* by Charles Sheldon. I remember how impressed I was with the integrity with which those new Christians made their decisions, and it affected my life for *good.* As mothers we can be wise in the kind of books and magazines our children have available to them.

We can "plant" good magazines in the bathroom and other strategic locations. We can provide magazines such as *Youth Alive* and *Woman's Touch,* as well as books and other good Christian reading materials. Our children are guided by what they read.

First Timothy 5:22 says, "Keep thyself pure." This is a command. We are responsible to be good and upright. If we read 2 Timothy 3:1-7 it almost sounds like the headlines of the evening paper. Evil abounds and makes people "despisers of those who are good."

I cringe when I see young people poking fun at Christian youth who take their stand for the right. They berate them. "Pansy, you don't smoke—don't drink—don't swear—don't use drugs." Our children need special prayer in these evil days to withstand the wickedness around them.

We have a young friend who was open in her Christian testimony and witness. The kids at school slipped drugs into her food a little at a time. One day she had a very bad trip that put her in the hospital and left her nearly a vegetable. Only the power of prayer finally made her a rational person.

The Occult

Can you pick up a secular magazine that doesn't have a horoscope column in it? Hardly. They vary a lot as to their content (and this should tell us something), yet there are women who live completely by what the stars indicate.

We were with a tour group. When they were introduced, instead of giving their names, they said, "I'm Scorpio—I'm Aries—I'm Pisces—" actually forming new friends by their sign of the zodiac. We need to be careful to shun the very appearance of evil.

Pornography and homosexuality are blatantly aired over television and available in magazines for all to see. We must be wise and teach our children to choose the good. We must shun all experimentation in evil. May God help us to raise up a standard against the evil one to save our homes.

"Surely goodness and mercy shall follow me all the days of my life: And I will dwell in the house of the Lord forever" (Psalm 23:6).

Exploring Together

1. Whom do you know that you consider a "good" person?
2. Are we afraid for people to think that we are good? Why?
3. How does goodness grow? (Ephesians 5:9.)
4. What are some of the things that tempt you to do evil?
5. Write down some area in which you need help in prayer. You might share this in your group and pray for each other. After 2 weeks have testimonies about ways God is helping you with your problem.

CHAPTER EIGHT

Faith

Lois and Eunice
Our Godly Heritage

2 TIMOTHY 1:1-14

Could it be possible that you are raising a great minister at your table? What will be the lasting effect of your personality upon each member of your family after he leaves home?

Each day has two handles—one is anxiety, one is faith. The one you grasp depends on you. I can hear my mother as each morning she would send us off to school with the prayer, "We apply the blood of Jesus to our doorposts and to our entire lives today." We lived with faith, under the canopy of God's protection each day.

Natural Faith

"The fruit of the Spirit is . . . faith." Faith is the product of absorbing the Word of God and believing His promises. Everyone has some faith. When you sit down on a chair you have faith it will hold you. When you drive your car you have faith you will arrive at your destination. When you buy food and prepare it you have faith that there will be no poison in it. This is a natural everyday faith, but we will see how God wants the fruit of faith to be an integral part of our nature and our life garden.

The Word says that without faith it is impossible to please God. God is love, so once again we see how the fruit of the Spirit are all interrelated. For the fruit to grow we start with love, but fruit continues to grow in our lives by faith.

You Never Say, "No"

During one of our furloughs I was teaching two subjects at a Bible college while working on my last year toward my own degree. The pastor asked me to start a young married couples class which was badly needed at the local church. I felt that with my studies, family, and teaching I had my hands more than full. I was already washing clothes at midnight. We were talking it over at the table at home when my son said, "But, Mommy, I've never known you to turn down an opportunity."

There was my answer. He had faith that by faith I could do it and the Lord would help me. And He did. There may be times when "No" is the right answer, but that time it was not for me.

What Does the Word Say?

1. Romans 10:17—"Faith cometh by hearing, and hearing by the Word."
   Faith is the natural product of absorbing the Word of God and believing His promises. But you can hear the Word preached without profit if you don't mix it with faith (Hebrews 4:2).
2. 1 Corinthians 13:12, 13—Faith is an unmovable confidence. It abides in us; it is part of us.
3. Luke 1:37—"For with God nothing shall be impossible." Faith operates in the sphere of the impossible. Where we can see, feel, and touch, we don't need faith. Faith is believing, trusting, and knowing without seeing.
4. Hebrews 11:1-6—Faith is confidence. It is substance. We can be sure. Faith is not an option.

"Without faith it is impossible to please God."

5. Mark 9:23—"All things are possible to him that believeth."

Faith operates by obedience to spiritual laws. Christianity is more than a philosophy, more than theology, more than polemics; it is a science. Science is a body of truth that is based on a proven formula. Jesus is the basis of truth for our faith. We can know the truth as we put our trust in Him. It works.

6. Hebrews 11:8-11—Abraham was a faithful man. He was called, he obeyed, he went out, he waited, he looked for a city, and he believed without seeing.

7. 2 Corinthians 5:7—"For we walk by faith and not by sight."

So on I go not knowing,
I would not if I might
I'd rather walk in the dark by faith,
Than to go alone by sight.

Almost every woman's magazine today carries articles about problems in homes and marriages. These problems are not new. Many people have the idea that all the marriages in the Bible were perfect. But we have seen Hannah's situation with two wives in the home. We know that Timothy grew up in a divided home.

Timothy's mother Eunice and his grandmother Lois were Jewish, but his father was a Gentile. This meant that the burden of teaching and training Timothy rested on these two women. It was a marriage with problems—divided in faith, customs, culture, and religious background. Paul calls Timothy his son in the faith, which indicates he also guided and prayed for him every day.

Unfeigned Faith

Paul tells Timothy the thing that he really remembers about him is his unfeigned faith, which stemmed from his grandmother Lois and his mother Eunice.

What is unfeigned faith? Faith that is genuine. It is sincere faith. The word *sincere* comes from Latin or Italian. Some of today's most outstanding marble sculptors are Italian. Outside the shops selling their statues you can see a sign: "Estatuas Sin Cera." "These statues don't have any wax in them." Thus, you know the white pearly marble in those statues is first-class.

In Paul's day, in the second-grade statues, if there were an imperfection in the marble, as the artisan was chiseling he would fill the area with white wax. It couldn't be detected with the eye.

If you put this kind of figurine in your yard and the rain came, the sun beat down, the hail began to pound, and the snow blew, what would happen to the wax? Yes, it would melt in the sun and crack away in the cold. You'd have an imperfect statue. So Paul uses this beautiful word *sincere* to describe Timothy's faith. "Your faith has no wax in it. Rain or shine, adversity or joy, your faith does not waver."

Faith is not put on the outside as a cloak to wear to church and then take off during the week. "Timothy, your faith is like your mother's faith, it is sincere, real, genuine faith."

No Good to Die By

Shortly before we left Argentina I heard that my friend Pilar, whose husband was the choir director in the American High School in Buenos Aires, was suffering from cancer. I heard she was going to be at a certain concert and I felt I should go to make a new contact with her. I had tried 5 years earlier, but she wasn't ready then. She was a self-contained, agnostic philosophy teacher and felt she had all her tomorrows arranged, organized, and under control.

I prayed with her in the gymnasium after the choir sang and said I would visit her Tuesday. When I went to her apartment I opened the downstairs door with the keys she tossed to me from the balcony above. After climbing the stairs, I found her seated on four pillows, waiting for me.

She said, "Betty Jane, to tell you that I needed you was the hardest thing I have ever done in all my life. I've never needed anyone. I have been in complete control of my life. My philosophy was good to live by, but now I am afraid. It is not enough to die by."

Then she told me how she realized she needed to find someone with faith. "Philosophy serves to live— but not to die." She said, "I passed the faces of all my friends through my memory—teachers, philosophers, historians, educators, administrators, family, politicians, and finally the one face that came to me was yours. Yours was the only face with faith."

How important it is to live our faith. Someone will need it. Pilar and I read the Bible together. Week after week I returned. She said, "Yes, I understand now He's knocking at the door of my heart. I'm not ready to open the door, but I have hold of His sleeve so He won't go away."

Pilar finally accepted Christ and began to grow in the Word. As I visited her every week and we prayed together, she became stronger and was able to go to church with me. She was baptized in water. During Easter week, as I laid my hand on her, she burst out speaking in a bubbling, beautiful new tongue in the Holy Spirit. Her agnostic life was completely transformed.

Just 1 month after we left her, her husband Walter

wrote that she had gone to be with the Lord. He said that although she had suffered a great deal because of a doctor's error in puncturing her lung in a drainage, her face was transformed with such light and beauty. So in her death she was more of a testimony to her unbelieving friends than in her life.

He wrote, "Now I too must believe in eternal life." And he has followed the faith that shone from her life.

The world is weary, dying, and looking for answers. We must live and show forth the fruit of faith in our lives. Our sincere, unfeigned faith is the answer to the doubts and fears of a world without faith.

"You've Studied the Scriptures"

Paul thanks God for this young man who accepted Christ as a youth. He writes to him as a son to encourage him to grow in the faith that is so evident in his home. In 2 Timothy 3:15 he reminds Timothy that he has studied the Scriptures since he was a child, and that they are able to make him wise through faith.

Here we see the importance of studying the Bible together at home. It is the source Book for all our decisions, for our way of life. Actually, many people are lost today. They don't have a model to measure themselves by. They have no moral norms or basis for conscience—for deciding what is right and wrong. We must go back to the Book. It must be the level that we lay our lives on to see if the little bubble says straight and upright or off-center and crooked.

Lay Your Hands on Your Child

Paul says, "Stir up the gift of God which I imparted to you when I laid my hands on you." Mother, have you laid gentle hands on your child and prayed over him? I feel it is very important for you to accompany your child to the altar and put your arm around him to let him feel your closeness and know that you love him and are imparting God's faith as you pray with him.

Verse 7 says, "For God hath not given us the spirit of fear; but of power, and of love, and of a sound mind." Where there is fear, faith can't grow. We must realize that fear doesn't come from God. We must keep ourselves from fear. God gives us power, love, and a sound mind. This is the essence of faith. Only in faith can you give your testimony, live a pure life, and follow the calling and purpose of God for your life.

What Have You Committed?

My mother repeated verse 12 each day, "For I know whom I have believed, and am persuaded that he is able to keep that which I have committed unto him against that day." This is the fruit of faith—to know whom we have believed and to know that He is able to keep all we've committed to Him. The complete fruition of faith in our lives will be when we see Jesus.

Timothy went with Paul on his missionary journeys. Lois and Eunice had to let him go. They knew they had trained him, taught him, and prayed with him. Now it was time for him to fulfill the purpose for which God had called and anointed him.

I remember waving good-bye to my parents as they stood at the gate each time we left to return to South America as missionaries. I remember when we left our own 17-year-old son standing at the Minneapolis airport in a yellow shirt, waving good-bye. He looked like a little canary—so young, pure, and vulnerable. But he was entering Bible college to fulfill God's plan for his life and we needed to go back to our ministry, as in Acts 20:24, to fulfill with joy the ministry the Lord had laid out for us.

We waved so bravely and then fixed our faces to the window of the airplane as the tears rolled down our cheeks. "But I *know* that all I have committed unto You, You will keep." This is a wonderful faith to live by, this constant confidence.

We committed everything to the Lord. Now we see it all working out. As I write this book, Rocky and Sherry are preparing to go as missionaries. But we had to commit them and hold on with light fingers, not grasping and withdrawing.

All Part of the Package

Mona Re' wrote us from Panama. "Mommy, they are inviting me to stay to teach in the two Bible schools here. They need teachers so badly. I feel like I'm jumping over a high cliff and there's no one below to catch me. I must make my decision today." She broke her contract to teach Spanish at the Bible college, gave up her apartment and also her engagement. It was all part of the package.

When she wrote she didn't have any money to buy stamps for her letters, we wrote asking what she was living on? "Faith, Mommy."

"But you can't eat faith, someone will help you."

"Mommy, where did I learn it?"

The very essence of your home can instill faith in the face of every problem. I was a small child when my father had a gall bladder attack with pain, chills, and fever. Mother called us children around the bed and we all prayed with that pure faith of a child. My father is 84 years old and still praising God today for the help received.

What you do talks so loudly
That I can't hear what you say.

What kind of faith do you serve with the hamburgers at your table? Is it "sincere" faith with no wax in it? In problems, sickness, decisions, and trials, sincere faith can survive. It is pure and immovable. This is the faith of God that abides. It is the fruit of the Spirit that grows in our life garden.

Put the Sign up in Your Kitchen

A woman with three children told an evangelist she felt she would like to have a ministry. The evangelist said, "Come back tomorrow night, I will help you." The next night she went to him again. "Here, you take this poster home and put it up in your kitchen," he said.

She looked at it:

>"Sacred services are celebrated
>Three times a day in this place."

Can we grasp the full meaning of this? As we prepare those three meals each day, wash the dishes, and do what seems to be routine, we are actually celebrating and having divine services! If we are ministering in faith and love and doing everything as unto the Lord, our kitchen is a holy place.

We must abide in the Vine. As we dwell in the presence of our Lord, as we continue in the Word and abide in Him, faith permeates our whole life and thinking. And it goes from the kitchen out to others.

Our Godly Heritage—You Choose

I'm glad that as I grew up my parents allowed me to make my own choices. Sometimes this makes choosing harder. Young people find it easier to say, "My church is against that," or, "My parents won't let me." But my father used to say, "You know how we have trained you, now you choose." This is an important part of our godly heritage.

We must be able to trust our children to make the correct decisions. And if they make a mistake and choose wrong, we must have faith in them and love and back them. If we keep living the example of faith in front of our children, they will be conscious of wrong choices. Faith will help them rectify mistakes.

To have faith is to trust and obey even when we don't understand. I once heard Dr. Robert Spence, the president of Evangel College, say, "When God called me, it wasn't any effort for me to obey. I had learned as a child not to cry and whine and kick when my father spoke. So it was easy to obey God."

Obey Without Making a Face

When Rocky graduated from high school we were ready to leave for Argentina. The district brethren informed us that he had been named "Mr. CA USA" for 1970. They asked us to come to the Minnesota camp meeting where they would announce this honor. It was to be a complete surprise to Rocky.

The day was warm and even many of the ministers had their jackets off. We were on the platform with the missionary group. I noticed Rocky in the audience with his jacket off. I caught his eye and made a movement of putting on my jacket. He watched me, took his coat, and quietly slipped into it. Just then Brother G. Raymond Carlson said, "Mr. CA USA was president of his soccer team."

The light dawned on Rocky's face as he realized it would be his name they would call. He hadn't grimaced, made a face, or shaken his head when I signaled him to put on his jacket. He had obeyed and now was ready to come forward to receive the honor.

To my heart this is the fulfillment of faith—to be able to trust and obey, without understanding.

As for Me and My House We Will Serve God

Grandpa Grams emigrated to the States from Germany in 1909. When he decided to read the Bible and follow the teachings of the Book, his beer-drinking friends left him. He chose the path of faith. He had 12 children, all serving God and preaching the gospel with their lives. With the grandchildren, we now number 100 who are guarding the faith entrusted to us.

Be not dismayed whate'er betide
God will take care of you.

An Encounter With Truth

1. How can we make sure that faith is growing in our life gardens?
2. Can your children follow your example?
3. Are you able to keep faith even in a problem?
4. Do you pray with your children?
5. Have you ever laid your hands on them to pray?
6. Are you implanting a bulwark of faith in their lives?
7. Can you trust your children to make wise choices?
8. How can you guide them without interfering?
9. What things tend to move you away from faith?
10. What is the purpose of your life?
11. What is the thing that drives you?
12. What is the most important thing in your life?
13. Do you spend more time on other things than on guiding your children?
14. Do your neighbors know you have faith? How?
15. How do you face life when things don't go easy for you? What is your attitude?
16. How can your faith be increased?

CHAPTER NINE

Meekness

Hagar, It Costs to Obey

GENESIS 16

"There's that word *meek* again. I don't want to be meek. People will think I'm stupid," said my friend Pilar.

She was beginning to read the Bible with me. She was looking at it with the fresh eye of an innocent child, although she was a well-educated, agnostic philosophy teacher.

"I want to assert myself, have my own way, stand for my rights, and establish my worth. I can't afford to be meek. That will ruin what I've accomplished as a woman; people will step on me."

"No, Pilar, Jesus sets the example for us. He says, 'Come unto me, all ye that labor and are heavy laden, and I will give you rest. Take my yoke upon you, and learn of me; for I am meek and lowly in heart: and ye shall find rest unto your souls.' Jesus is our Example. He says He will bear the other side of the yoke."

"You have seen the carts pulled in the sandy streets by the oxen? How do they use the yoke?"

"Over two oxen."

"Can you put a yoke over an ox and a tall mule?"

"No, the mule is too haughty and high-spirited. They are not equal."

"Or over a donkey and an ox?"

"No—too stubborn and low. He won't budge. I'm beginning to see. But it's not easy."

105

Meek Is Not Weak

"The fruit of the Spirit is . . . meekness." To be meek is to have quiet power, courage, dignity of character; to be strong, yet humble. Jesus said, "Come . . . learn of me . . . take my yoke."

I love the verbs of the Bible. They help me to know the steps to follow Jesus' way. He takes our stubborn, rebellious, antagonistic spirit and teaches us to wear His yoke. You cannot bend the neck without bowing the head. He's on the other side. Step, step, step—walking with Jesus, learning of Him.

The Bible tells us in Numbers 12:6 that Moses was the meekest man who ever lived. We studied how Jochebed instilled peace in him through her nature. He was highly prepared in the universities of Egypt. He had royal authority and training as a lawyer and administrator. Yet, Moses chose to go with the humble Hebrews and be part of them, rather than become the king of Egypt.

Moses went up into Mt. Sinai to commune with God for 40 days. His face was transformed and shining. As he came down the mountain he heard the noise of a wild party. "What's happening?" He saw the big golden bull Apis, the famous god of Egypt. All the people were dancing and reveling.

Aaron said the women had brought their golden bracelets and nose rings and he had tossed them into the fire. Then, like magic, out jumped a gold calf from the flame! Godly Moses grabbed a hammer and beat the image into powder. Then he sprinkled the gold on the water and made everyone drink it. He was meek, yet full of strength and authority.

When Aaron and Miriam criticized his choice of a wife and caused discord among the 3 million Hebrews, leprous sores began to erupt on Miriam's body. Instead of saying, "Well, you asked for it. It serves you right. Suffer it out!'' Moses went to God and prayed for her. He said, ''I love you, Miriam, we'll wait right here in the desert until you are well.''

Let's look again at 1 Corinthians 13 and list some of the phrases describing love:

Does not insist on its own way
Does not pursue selfish advantage
Is not anxious to impress
Is not resentful
Doesn't have inflated ideas of its own importance
Is not puffed up
Does not gloat over others' misfortune
Does not answer back
In honor preferring one another

Actually this sounds like the fruit of meekness, doesn't it? Meekness is unselfish, does not push ahead in the line at the supermarket, does not elbow others out of the way, prefers others above herself, and takes what's left without complaint. Meekness is a close relative of love!

How Can I Forgive?

Corrie ten Boom tells how after her release from the concentration camp in Germany, she was speaking at different churches about forgiveness.

One night as she looked into the audience, she recognized the face of one of the Nazi guards who had been instrumental in the beating that caused the death of her sister Betsie. She thought, ''How can I forgive him?''

At the close of the meeting he came to her. ''Madam, I would like to ask your forgiveness for all the wrong we did. You are now my sister in Jesus.''

He extended his hand to her. But she stuffed hers

into her purse, pretending to hunt for a hanky. She couldn't bring herself to shake his hand. She couldn't forgive him. Then she heard a Voice, "Forgive us even as we forgive others. Forgive us even as we forgive others. If we do not forgive, then our Father in heaven doesn't forgive."

She pulled her hand out of her purse and thrust it into his extended hand. The joy of pardon linked them by the Spirit. The Nazi guard and the Dutch Christian were brought together in forgiveness. We learn meekness by suffering.

The Pruning Shears

For the fruit of meekness to grow we need to use the pruning shears we brought to class the first day. We will have to lop off some of our own ways and attitudes that we may have allowed to grow in our garden. This is going to hurt. It will be surgery.

A. Examples of meekness
   1. Moses was meek—Numbers 12:3
   2. Jesus was meek—Matthew 11:28-30
B. Portrait of meekness
   Titus 2:3-10—strength in all our character
C. Meekness is manifested in the Word
   1. Our attitude before God—1 Timothy 6:11
      Follow faith, love, patience, meekness.
   2. Restore those who are fallen—Galatians 6:1, 2
      In the spirit of meekness, bear their problems.
   3. Receive God's Word with meekness—James 1:21
   4. How should we testify?—1 Peter 3:15
   5. What is the basis of our charm?—1 Peter 3:4
   6. How to do the work of a pastor—2 Timothy 2:24, 25
   7. How should we walk?—Ephesians 4:1-3

8. How can we forgive?—Ephesians 4:26, 32
9. How to humble ourselves—Mark 11:25

Meekness is the spirit of patience working in our character to make us gentle, loving, kind, and pliable. In our study of "gentleness" we looked at the shepherd song in Isaiah 42. We need to remember that gentleness and meekness are twins.

Not "Good Riddance"

Edgar was a very talented young man in our church. He was a Sunday school teacher and the president of the youth department. He would come a half hour late to teach his class, forget to bring his materials, and be arrogant in his manner. He was always threatening to quit. One day he said he had received a scholarship to study in Russia and was giving up everything.

It would have been so easy to say, "Great, good riddance of a continuous problem." But just then God gave a special portion of meekness to my German husband. He said, "Let's just take a moment to pray about it here in the classroom." That quiet bit of meekness broke Edgar's heart and he wept like a baby. He began to allow meekness to grow in his own life and became a valuable worker.

Walk Worthy

In Ephesians 4:1-3 we are told to walk in lowliness, meekness, and long-suffering, worthy of our high calling. What is this calling? To be kings, priests, queens, royal ministers—a holy nation before God. We don't have to defend ourselves. We don't have to answer back. My father used to say, "If you live right, your life will betray anyone who is speaking falsely against you."

109

Your Fault

The advice in Ephesians 4:26 is very important to our growth in meekness. We must learn to ask forgiveness.

Many people allow tension in their home to destroy their marriage. There were more than a million divorces in America in 1975. And one of the casualties was Ann Landers! You've probably read her usually wise words of counsel in the newspaper. Yet, in 1975 her marriage of 36 years was dissolved. To be able to counsel is not enough.

One of the decisions Monnie and I made before we were married was never to use the words, "your fault," in our home. We have seen many good marriages disintegrate for a lack of meekness. The Bible speaks of submission on the part of the wife in marriage, and it also says the husband should love, cherish, and protect his wife.

There are many situations that demand meekness in a marriage. Have you heard some of these statements?

"You're never around when the children need you."

"You dominate me."

"I resent your interference."

"I hate to come home. I don't have a moment's peace."

"I don't think you're fair, I have to do everything."

"Why don't you quit nagging? You make me tired."

"You never do this. . . ."

You Never—You Never—

"You never pick up your clothes."

"You never put the cap back on the toothpaste."

"You never turn out the lights."

"You never clean out your pockets."

"You never—*ad infinitum.*"

"In honor preferring one another."

After a certain man and his wife had an angry disagreement, he put a board down the center of their double bed to separate them. Each night they slept like saints, guarding the bitterness in their hearts.

One night they heard a message on forgiveness at a rally. Each of them felt impressed to be reconciled to the other, ask forgiveness, and start anew. When they went to bed that night the wife moved over a little, thinking to open communications. He said, "You pushed the board."

"No, I didn't."

"Yes, you did. It fell on me—you did it on purpose." And the whole ugly ulcer broke open again. It took a long time to heal because meekness was not evident in their relationship.

It seems ridiculous and it is funny, but it's actually a true story. Don't let the sun go down on your wrath. This is a good practice. Be submissive. Give in. Bow your neck; ask forgiveness. You'll see how it will heal situations. It takes two people to fight.

Pouting

My father was a tender, gentle person. We had a happy peaceful home. He told how his own parents used to fight. They would blame each other for their problems. They would eat at the same table and sleep in the same bed, yet not speak to each other for weeks at a time. They kept a running feud of silence going.

We need to know how to be quiet without clamming up. We must keep communications open and talk things over in meekness.

Meekness—Homemade Jam

Meekness is probably the fruit of the Spirit that is most necessary at home. A father came home one night and saw the lawn hadn't been cut and their big dog had made a hole in the fence. It hadn't been fed and was without water. He grabbed his belt and whipped the first boy he met.

"But, Daddy, it wasn't my turn to take care of the dog, this was Bob's week," he sobbed.

What should that father have done? Colossians 3:21 says parents shouldn't scold so much that their children give up. We need to ask forgiveness. David Wilkerson's book *Parents on Trial* shows the need of meekness.

After I disciplined Rachel, I would slip in by her bed, put my arm around her, and say, "Now, let's pray together about it." We teach meekness by being submissive and kind.

It Costs to Ask Forgiveness

"No, I'm not ready to be baptized yet," Isidora told us.

"But you've taken the doctrine class for new converts four times and you've been saved for several years."

"Yes," she said, "That's true, but I'm not ready." And she lowered her eyes.

I missed her at several of the women's meetings, which she had always faithfully attended. Two months later she returned and her face was beaming. "When is the next baptismal service?" she asked. Then she told me her story.

When she was 18 years old she was deceived and abused by a Spanish landowner in her village. Her father was furious. He fought with her and she ran away to the big city. She had two children by the landowner and was raising them alone. She worked hard for them. She had never returned home, and she didn't even know if her parents were living.

Finally, after she was saved, in the spirit of meekness she left on a big truck piled high with lumber and flour. She rode along the winding roads up over the snow-covered mountains in the glacier area of the Andes Mountains. It took 3 days to get to her village. She found her parents, told them about Christ, asked their forgiveness, and thus pulled up the roots of bitterness that had grown in her soul for over 25 years. Now she was back and she knew she could follow the Lamb and be baptized.

They've Abused Me

Hagar was running away. She just couldn't take another day of Sarah's abuse. For 10 years she had faithfully served Sarah since they had left her homeland of Egypt. She was tall and beautiful, dark and graceful. Pharaoh had given her to Sarah as a present when they left after the famine. Now she was carrying Abraham's child at Sarah's encouragement. Sarah wanted Abraham to have a son as the angel had promised. If her servant bore a son she could call him her own.

But Hagar had become arrogant and disobedient after she had conceived. Jealousy and animosity grew between the two women. Sarah was demanding more work, and Hagar was retaliating by being slow and arrogant. Then Sarah couldn't stand the conflict any longer and she "dealt hardly with her."

Hagar yanked off her slave apron and ran away. But where could she go? She had always been clever in the desert, but now the night was all black. Had the stars moved? She felt the sand in her teeth. The night sounds were not reassuring.

Lost

She was lost. She must have been walking in circles. She was so tired. Her body, heavy with child, was uncomfortable. Should she just give up? She could commit suicide. Ten years gone from her people, and now she was lost, tired, hungry, and blue. Her foot hit something. She fell in a heap in the desert. She couldn't go any further.

Where Are You Going?

"Hagar, Sarah's maid," a voice called. Who could know her? Who knew her name? Who knew her position? Then the angel of the Lord asked her, "Where did you come from, and where are you going?"

Take note of the precision of God's questions. God always gives man an opportunity to declare himself.

"Adam, where are you?" "I'm back here in my tailor shop making a fig-leaf suit."

"Cain, where is your brother?"

"Hagar, where are you going?" She could have lied. She could have hedged. But she told the truth. "I am running away."

"Where are you going?"

"I don't know."

How many have to answer today, "I am running away." You cannot hide from God; His eye is fixed on you in love. You take your worst enemy along when you run.

"Go back. Go back and submit yourself to Sarah. Obey; do as she tells you. You will have a boy. His name will be Ishmael, which means, 'God hears.' "

The eternal omnipotent God of all the universe knew about Hagar. He called her by name. He knew her need. He saw her rebellion. And He found her when she was lost. He spoke to her and made her a promise. "Now go back, Hagar, and ask pardon; submit yourself."

Hagar thought it over—her options weren't too great. It was better to obey.

Knock, knock, knock—

"Who is it?"

"I have returned, my lady. I will obey. Forgive me. Take me in. Give me another chance. I will serve you."

Hagar called the well where the angel had found her, "Beer-lahai-roi," which means, "The well of him who lives and sees me."

Have you fallen by the well? Do you feel discouraged? Is it hard to humble yourself and submit? Are there too many things to make right? God *sees* you! He knows your name. He knows your need. He knows your rebellion. He knows the whole situation. Don't be afraid to humble yourself in meekness. He will come to you. He will speak to you and bring healing and restoration.

It must have cost Hagar a great deal to submit and find the spirit of meekness.

> *I am lost if you take your hand from me,*
> *I am blind, oh, Lord please help me see;*
> *Let me always ever thy servant be*
> *Lead me, oh, Lord lead me;*
> *Lead me, guide me along life's way.*

Following His Footsteps

1. How do we fulfill the law of meekness where we work?
2. If we are meek will we be abused?
3. What did Jesus mean when He said, "I am meek and lowly"?
4. How can we demonstrate meekness in our homes?
5. Are you stubborn?

6. Do you demand your own way?

7. Do you pout?

8. Hebrews 12:6 refers to the root of bitterness. Who could be affected by your bitterness?

9. What should we do if we have offended our child?

10. Have you watched the shoulders of someone who has been offended? What happens? What about his face?

11. What does "aught against any" in Mark 11:25 mean?

12. Do you handle emergencies or a change in plans as a woman of grace?

CHAPTER TEN

Temperance

Ruth, The Choice Is up to You
Self-control in Decisions

RUTH 1 to 4

The growth of the fruit of the Spirit in our lives is a composite. We can't say, "I'm just going to grow a 'joy orchard' or a 'goodness grove.'" When our life in the Spirit begins, we find the fruit is like a cluster of grapes, each one perfect—but all in a cluster.

So when love begins to grow we will find peace, joy, and goodness developing too. And next to these will be growing temperance or self-control, the last of our ninefold fruit.

Growth in the Spirit depends on our wanting to grow and preparing the climate for growth within our lives. But no amount of effort will help us develop these nine fruit without walking in the Spirit, for they are the "fruit of the Spirit."

Plastic

In one home we visited, the family had many decorator items—trees, flowers, and a fountain. Our 5-year-old was quite impressed. Then he walked over to touch them and said, "They're just plastic, Mommy." We live in a plastic age, but may the fruit in our life garden be real—the kind that can reproduce!

More Than Drinking

"The fruit of the Spirit is . . . temperance." We

usually think of temperance in connection with liquor and drinking. And it is true that many women are drinking in their lonely private hours. They need help. Many articles have been written about the problem of alcoholism among women. I feel we need to teach our children that "he who takes not the first cup will never fill a drunkard's grave." But that is only one area where temperance is needed.

For us, a whole world is opened by the thought of temperance, for it means "self-control." It means internal strength to control our impulses, govern our desires, and guard our attitudes and passions—to actually be our own person and be in control of our decisions.

I have known the following verse since childhood:

> I have to live with myself and so,
> I want to be fit for myself to know.
> I want to be able as the days go by
> To stand up and look myself in the eye.

Can we control ourselves? Or is there some part of our life we can't govern?

First Corinthians 6:12 says: "As a Christian I *may* do anything, but that does not mean that everything is good for me to do. I may do everything, but I must not be a slave of anything" *(Phillips)*.

Moderation in everything includes controlling our physical, mental, and spiritual appetites. It calls for self-control in the use of time, the way we dress, and our manner of speaking. We can go to extremes in joking, anger, derision, "clean fun," or criticism. Moderation, or temperance, is needed in eating habits, attitudes, uses of leisure, and sexual desires.

I love the thought in 2 Timothy 1:7 that God has given us a sound mind. This is a great gift. With a sound mind we can make the right choices and be able to govern our thoughts and impulses. We should thank God each day for the right use of our minds.

The possibility of choice, to make our own decisions is a great benefit in being a Christian. It develops Christian character. Socrates' wife Xanthippe had a very bad temper. Someone asked him, "Why don't you teach her?"

Socrates answered, "My aim in life is to get on well with people. I chose Xanthippe because I knew if I could get along with her, I could get along with anyone."

He accepted a challenge. We are more prone to shun those who are difficult to get along with. We tend to like those who are like us. If another woman does things different from the way we do, we think she is strange.

We studied Titus 2 in the chapter on goodness. Take a good look and see how applicable it is for self-control too.

Your Time

"Time is the stuff life's made of," Benjamin Franklin said. So how do you control your time? We need to make a conscious effort to use it wisely and not waste it. Keep a pencil near your Bible to make notes as God impresses you. Read good books and absorb and fill your life with wholesome ideas. Learn to crochet, do gardening, or play the piano. Develop new skills.

We should be in control of our day. I make a list for each day, but sometimes evening comes and my list is still full. Does this happen to you? We "major in minors."

We need to be in control of our telephone time. Keep your sewing basket nearby. Fix the cuffs on those slacks, sew on those buttons. Keep your family's clothes in repair. Utilize those moments you might normally lose while riding in the car, talking on the phone, or watching TV.

And remember the television has an on-and-off control. There are programs today that aren't worth anyone's time. They shouldn't be allowed in our homes. The program that is gross, crude, laughs at everything sacred, and makes fun of all that should be respected, does not merit our time. We must exercise self-control and turn the knob.

Contentment

Philippians 4:11 says, "I have learned to be content." No one is born contented. As soon as the new baby is born his little head is moving, his mouth is making sucking motions, and his hands are grabbing. We are all born hunting and grabbing.

We must *learn* contentment—with a little or a lot, full or hungry. Many women nag, gripe, growl, and fuss. We must govern our attitudes. Our family learned to be content with cobblestone streets, mud-brick huts, and "running water," even when we had to run after it! Our hands and ears were chapped and cracked, but contentment made the difference.

Be Clever With Your Money

Good stewardship is a facet of temperance. Learn to buy things on sale instead of griping that your money doesn't stretch. Buy summer shoes at the close of summer, and winter shoes in the spring for the next season. Stretch your budget by shopping at garage sales. Watch for good brands. You can dress well and have some extra money for missions. I buy shirts during the after-Christmas inventory sales. I feel God guides me in these practical ways to better stewardship.

Don't Waste

If you have leftover bread, toast it in the oven, dust it with garlic salt, and make your own topping for a chef salad. Or roll stale bread with a rolling pin to make crumbs for meatballs, fried fish, or a topping for scalloped potatoes. I've seen some women throw away all their leftover bread and then buy packages of bread crumbs!

Teach your children how to manage money. They can learn to mow the lawn, carry out the garbage, and sweep the driveway because they are part of the family. Chores may also be linked to their weekly allowance. Proverbs 10:22 tells us: "The blessing of the Lord, it maketh rich, and he addeth no sorrow with it."

Take time to laugh together. Keep a sense of humor in your home. A light heart and laughter will carry you through many problems. First Timothy 6:6 reminds us, "Godliness with contentment is great gain."

Govern Your Tongue

1. James 3:2-11—Who can govern the tongue? It kindles a great fire. Don't say everything that comes to mind. Learn to be quiet.

2. Proverbs 16:32—"He that is slow to anger is better than the mighty; and he that ruleth his spirit than he that taketh a city." Control yourself.

3. Proverbs 17:1—"A dry crust eaten in peace is better than steak every day along with argument and strife" (Living Bible).

4. Proverbs 15:17—"It is better to eat soup with someone you love than steak with someone you hate" (Living Bible).

5. Proverbs 15:1—"A soft answer turneth away

wrath but grievous words stir up anger. . . . A wholesome tongue is a tree of life."

6. Proverbs 16:23, 24—"The heart of the wise teacheth his mouth, and addeth learning to his lips. Pleasant words are as an honey comb, sweet to the soul, and health to the bones."

Many are concerned with health foods—nuts, special seeds, brown rice, raw sugar, etc. The Word tells us the best health food is guarding our words and our thoughts.

> *Oh, to live above with saints we love*
> *That will be glory.*
> *But to live below with saints we know—*
> *That's another story!*

A Three-legged Stool

Marriage is like a three-legged stool. Our spiritual, emotional, and sexual natures are involved. For that stool to stand up, all three must be under control.

The first institution God created was the family. To make a woman, He took a bone from near the heart of Adam—to be loved and cherished; from under his arm—to be protected and to be his equal. Not from his foot to be trampled on, or from his head to dominate and subdue him. God's plan is good.

We have a sexual nature which is satisfied in marriage. Sex is not something to be snickered about and learned in dark alleys, but an open sharing love that fulfills all our nature. We must have a healthy approach toward sex. As parents, we are responsible to teach the purity of sex in our homes.

As women of grace, we need to be careful about the way we dress, the way we move, and the way we sit. To be discreet in our person, not offering temptation to a man's heart through the eye gate is very important. We are also responsible to teach our daughters along these lines.

The Battle of the Bulge

Just a word about temperance at the table. I think the women of our church are noted for being some of the world's best cooks. We have traveled in many states. I have Swedish friends who make delicious brownies filled with nuts, cherries, and whipped cream. We enjoy them, but our bodies are the temple of the Lord so we need to be temperate in our eating.

What about a person with a touchy gall bladder who eats peanuts, herring, pizza, and hot chili? He eats them and says, "I'm going to trust the Lord. The pastor will pray for me." He is tempting the Lord. Here is where we all need to weigh our progress in self-control. We must be in control of our eating as well as our drinking.

I Choose You and Your God

The story of Ruth begins in a foreign country. Naomi and Elimelech moved to Moab because of a great famine. They made a new home for themselves. Their two boys married Moabite girls and they lived in Moab for 10 years. Then all three of the men died. Life became difficult for the three widows. They may have sold their wedding gifts to pay their bills, and, in general, reduced their life-style. Finally, Naomi decided to "go back home."

The girls walked alongside Naomi but she encouraged them to leave her and return to their people. What would three widows do? So Orpah kissed Naomi and chose to go back to her own culture, religion, customs, and people. We don't hear any more about her.

But Ruth said, "Mother Naomi, I have decided to go with you. Your country, your customs, and your people will be mine. Wherever you go, I will go with you. I choose your God for my God." What did Ruth see in her mother-in-law's life to make such a decision?

Not Lazy

Early in the morning Ruth was out in the fields following the harvest. She wasn't afraid of hard work. Others noticed she was there from early until late without resting. When she came home at night she emptied her apron. "Look, Naomi, nearly a whole bushel of grain today!" (Take an apron to indicate work, and a black shawl to indicate her being a widow.)

Do you stand by the time clock waiting for it to click so you can punch out? Or do you serve with a generous attitude? Rebekah is another girl in the Bible who knew how to work. It made her Isaac's bride.

Guide Our Footsteps

Naomi said, "Where did you glean today?"

"In Boaz's field. He spoke to me."

"Ah," answered Naomi, "That is wonderful, for he is a kinsman. God is guiding our footsteps. Remember we prayed this morning and committed our steps and our day to God's care? It is possible Boaz will clear the title on our land. Then we will have some money to live on. Whatever he tells you to do, obey."

Ruth answered wisely. "I am a stranger here, whatever you tell me to do I will; I need your help."

Naomi told Ruth to go to the threshing floor and lie down by Boaz's feet while he was asleep. When Boaz found her he realized he could redeem their land

and make Ruth his wife. He guarded her purity and said he would help.

The ceremony was interesting. They called another closer relative before the civic court of 10 elders. He said his sons and wife wouldn't understand his receiving a Moabitess along with the property. So he gave his shoe to Boaz. "You go ahead and buy Elimelech's land! I won't be able to take Ruth."

Boaz had seen Ruth's kindness to her mother-in-law, her willingness to work, her grace, and her integrity of character. He accepted her at face value.

God's Recompense

Naomi had told Ruth, "Be patient, sit still, wait and see." That's hard sometimes. We want everything to move quickly. We want to see ahead. But Ruth was filled with self-control. God honored this. Ruth and Boaz had a baby boy. They named him Obed, which means "serving." Their baby became the grandfather of King David, which made Ruth, the former pagan, David's great-grandmother.

Psalm 46:10 says, "Be still and know that I am God, I will be exalted among the nations." I love the promise in Psalm 90:15-17 that God will prosper the work of our hands and make it to stand. But we must learn to quiet our natures, still our hearts, and be patient. God works everything out in His good time.

Ruth didn't see all this ahead in the future when she made her decision to go with Naomi. They were just two lonely widows walking along. But she chose well and God gave the recompense.

To grow in self-control is to grow in Christ. This growth isn't something remote and unreal, expressed in heavenly terms or cliches. To exercise self-control by the help of the Holy Spirit each day is to live a practical contemporary Christian life.

We are a heavenly people, but we must live here on earth. We need to bring heaven into our homes, our offices, and our schools, praying, "Out of my life, may Jesus shine."

No amount of self-improvement will be lasting unless it is the fruit growing through the Spirit's control. Thus, we grow in grace through the power of the Spirit in our lives. My prayer is that you may be a woman of grace; your life a fragrant, fruit-filled garden bringing blessings to your home, your church, your community, and your world.

Contentment

Life is but a span in the measure of years,
Fraught with many fears,
Laughter, joys, and tears.
Through it all our God is just waiting to bless.
Even in the wilderness, contented, I journey on.

Suggested Reading

Beardsley, Lou, and Toni Spry. *The Fulfilled Woman*. Irvine, CA: Harvest House Publishers, Inc., 1975.

Bennet, Rita. *I'm Glad You Asked That*. Plainfield, NJ: Logos International, 1974.

Brandt, Henry, and Phil Landrum. *I Want My Marriage to Be Better*. Grand Rapids: Zondervan Publishing House, 1976.

Brock, Raymond. *The Christ-centered Family*. Springfield, MO: Gospel Publishing House, Radiant Life Series, 1977.

LaHaye, Tim. *Spirit-controlled Temperament*. Wheaton, IL: Tyndale House Publishers, 1966.

Landorf, Joyce. *The Fragrance of Beauty*. Wheaton, IL: Victor Books, 1973.

Landorf, Joyce. *The Richest Lady in Town*. Grand Rapids: Zondervan Publishing House, 1973.

Mains, Karen B. *Open Heart—Open Home*. Elgin, IL: David C. Cook Publishing Co., 1976.

Miles, Judith. *The Feminine Principle*. Minneapolis: Bethany Fellowship, Inc., 1975.

Peale, Ruth. *The Adventure of Being a Wife*. New York: Fawcett World Library, 1976.

Price, Eugenia. *Woman to Woman*. Grand Rapids: Zondervan Publishing House, 1975.

Sanford, Agnes. *Healing Gifts of the Spirit*. New York: J. B. Lippincott Co., 1966.

Sanford, Agnes. *Sealed Orders: The Autobiography of a Christian Mystic*. Plainfield, NJ: Logos International, 1972.